THE JERUSALEM-HARVARD LECTURES

Sponsored by the Hebrew University of Jerusalem
and Harvard University Press

JEROME BRUNER

Acts of Meaning

HARVARD UNIVERSITY PRESS

Cambridge, Massachusetts
London, England

Copyright © 1990 by the President and Fellows
of Harvard College
All rights reserved
Printed in the United States of America
10 9 8 7 6 5 4

This book is printed on acid-free paper, and its binding
materials have been chosen for strength and durability.

Library of Congress Cataloging in Publication Data

Bruner, Jerome S. (Jerome Seymour)
Acts of meaning / Jerome Bruner.
p.   cm. — (The Jerusalem-Harvard lectures)
Includes bibliographical references and index.
ISBN 0-674-00360-8 (alk. paper)
1. Meaning (Psychology)
2. Cognitive psychology—History.
3. Ethnopsychology.
I. Title. II. Series.
BF455.B74   1990
150—dc20   90-40485
CIP

Designed by Gwen Frankfeldt

To Carol

Contents

Preface

Books are like mountaintops jutting out of the sea. Self-contained islands though they may seem, they are upthrusts of an underlying geography that is at once local and, for all that, a part of a universal pattern. And so, while they inevitably reflect a time and a place, they are part of a more general intellectual geography. This book is no exception.

I have written it at a time when psychology, the science of mind as William James once called it, has become fragmented as never before in its history. It has lost its center and risks losing the cohesion needed to assure the internal exchange that might justify a division of labor between its parts. And the parts, each with its own organizational identity, its own theoretical apparatus, and often its own journals, have become specialties whose products become less and less exportable. Too often they seal themselves within their own rhetoric and within their own parish of authorities. This self-sealing risks making each part (and the aggregate that increasingly constitutes psychology's patchquilt whole) ever more remote from other inquiries dedicated to the understanding of mind and the human condition—inquiries in the humanities or in the other social sciences.

There may be good reasons for what has happened, and perhaps it even reflects a needed "paradigm shift" in the human sciences. The "biological" side of psychology has abandoned its old base to join forces with the neurosciences. And the newly minted "cognitive sciences" have absorbed many of those who used to work in the vineyards of perception, memory, thinking, all of these now conceived as varieties of "information processing." These new alignments may be for the good: they could bring new and unexpected theoretical vigor to the task of understanding man.

But in spite of the splitting and fragmentation that seem to be occurring, I do not think either that psychology is coming to an end or that it is permanently condemned to live in segregated parishes. For psychology as an enterprise long predates its "official" conversion into a set of self-contained divisions. Its great questions are still alive. The founding of Wundt's "experimental" laboratory at Leipzig in 1879 did not cancel those questions; it only clothed them in new dress—the "new" positivist style so dear to the hearts of our late-nineteenth-century forebears. Even Wundt in his later years recognized how constricting the new "laboratory" style could be, and in formulating a "cultural psychology" urged that we embrace a more historical, interpretive approach to understanding man's cultural products.

We are still drawing rich sustenance from our more distant, pre-positivist past: Chomsky acknowledges his debt to Descartes, Piaget is inconceivable without Kant, Vygotsky without Hegel and Marx, and the once towering bastion of "learning theory" was constructed on foundations laid by John

Locke. And had Freud's followers fought free of the model of "bioenergetics" that was the shallowest aspect of his theory, psychoanalysis might have continued to grow in theoretical stature. The more recent cognitive revolution was inconceivable without the supporting philosophical climate of its time. And, indeed, if one looks beyond the boundaries of "official" psychology to our sister disciplines in the human sciences, one is struck by the lively renewal of interest in the classical questions raised in the century since Leipzig by Nietzsche and Peirce, by Austin and Wittgenstein, by Jakobson and de Saussure, by Husserl and Cassirer, by Foucault and Searle.

It is not surprising, then, that a reaction has set in against the narrowing and "sealing in" that are afflicting psychology. The wider intellectual community comes increasingly to ignore our journals, which seem to outsiders principally to contain intellectually unsituated little studies, each a response to a handful of like little studies. Inside psychology there is a worried restlessness about the state of our discipline, and the beginning of a new search for means of reformulating it. In spite of the prevailing ethos of "neat little studies," and of what Gordon Allport once called methodolatry, the great psychological questions are being raised once again—questions about the nature of mind and its processes, questions about how we construct our meanings and our realities, questions about the shaping of mind by history and culture.

And these questions, often pursued more vigorously outside than inside "official" psychology, are being reformulated with a subtlety and rigor that yield rich and generative answers. We know far better now how to approach the Great Comparisons whose resolutions have always challenged psychology: the comparison of man and his evolutionary forebears, man as immature child and man at full maturity, man in full health and man afflicted by mental illness or alienation, "human nature" as expressed in different cultures, and indeed even the comparison between man in flesh and blood with the machines constructed to simulate him. Each and every one of these inquiries has prospered when we have been willing to ask questions about such taboo topics as mind, intentional states, meaning, reality construction, mental rules, cultural forms, and the like. Occam's razor, warning us not to multiply our conceptual entities more than "necessary," was surely not intended to ban mind from the mental sciences. Nor were John Stuart Mill's principles of induction meant to quell all forms of intellectual curiosity save those which could be slaked by the controlled experiment.

This book is written against the background of psychology today, with its confusions, its dislocations, its new simplifications. I have called it *Acts of Meaning* in order to emphasize its major theme: the nature and cultural shaping of meaning-making, and the central place it plays in human action. It is not just an autobiographical quirk that I should be writing such a book now, though the reader will soon find that it "projects" my own long history as a psychologist. But all single voices are abstracted from dialogues, as Bakhtin teaches us. I have had the great good fortune to be a long-term participant in the dialogues that form and reform psychology. And what I shall have to say in the chapters that follow reflects my view of where the dialogue stands today.

This is not intended to be a "comprehensive" study of all and every aspect of the meaning-making process. That would be impossible in any case. Rather, it is an effort to illustrate what a psychology looks like when it concerns itself centrally with meaning, how it inevitably becomes a *cultural* psychology and how it must venture beyond the conventional aims of positivist science with its ideals of *reductionism, causal explanation* and *prediction*. The three need not be treated like the Trinity. For when we deal with meaning and culture, we inevitably move toward another ideal. To reduce meaning or culture to a material base, to say that they "depend," say, on the left hemisphere, is to trivialize both in the service of misplaced concreteness. To insist upon explanation in terms of "causes" simply bars us from trying to understand how human beings interpret their worlds and how *we* interpret *their* acts of interpretation. And if we take the object of psychology (as of any intellectual enterprise) to be the achievement of understanding, why is it necessary under all conditions for us to understand *in advance* of the phenomena to be observed—which is all that prediction is? Are not plausible interpretations preferable to causal explanations, particularly when the achievement of a causal explanation forces us to artificialize what we are studying to a point almost beyond recognition as representative of human life?

The study of the human mind is so difficult, so caught in the dilemma of being both the object and the agent of its own study, that it cannot limit its inquiries to ways of thinking that grew out of yesterday's physics. Rather, the task is so compellingly important that it deserves all the rich variety of insight that we can bring to the understanding of what man makes of his world, of his fellow beings, and of himself. That is the spirit in which we should proceed.

Acknowledgments

I CANNOT begin to mention all the people and institutions who shaped this book. For in many ways, it represents not only my most current thinking but also, as it were, a "return of the repressed." Some of the influences, consequently, are in the distant past, like the Department of Social Relations at Harvard where, for a decade beginning in the mid-1950s, I was nourished by the company of such as Clyde Kluckhohn and Gordon Allport, Talcott Parsons and Henry Murray. It was a department with a purpose, and each month we met as a seminar to elucidate that purpose: how to reconcile views of Man as a unique individual with views of him both as an expression of culture and as a biological organism. The debates of those Wednesday evenings reverberate in the pages that follow.

Then there was "Soc Sci 8," Conceptions of Man, in which George Miller and I tried to persuade a generation of Harvard and Radcliffe undergraduates that to know Man you must see him against the background of the animal kingdom from which he evolved, in the context of the culture and language that provide the symbolic world in which he lives, and in the light of the growth processes that bring these two powerful forces into concert. We had become convinced by then that psychology could not do the job on its own. And so we set up our own version of an interdisciplinary human science in General Education, and for most of the 1960s, from September through May each year, we managed to stay just a step ahead of our undergraduates.

And in the midst of this, the Center for Cognitive Studies was founded, about which much more will be said in the opening chapter. I mention it here only to express a debt to yet another community that helped convince me (by this time hardly against my will) that the boundaries that separated such fields as psychology, anthropology, linguistics, and philosophy were matters of administrative convenience rather than of intellectual substance.

Then there were those longtime conversational partners who constitute one's Generalized Other—George Miller, David Krech, Alexander Luria, Barbel Inhelder, Clifford Geertz, Albert Guerard, Roman Jakobson, Morton White, Elting Morison, David Olson. And still the list is incomplete, for I have left out my former students—from recent New York, through middle Oxford, to early Harvard.

Several friends read early drafts of this book and provided useful suggestions: Michael Cole, Howard Gardner, Robert Lifton, Daniel Robinson, and Donald Spence. I am very grateful for their help.

I owe an especial debt to my hosts in Jerusalem who, in December 1989, made life so thoroughly agreeable when I delivered the Jerusalem-Harvard Lectures at the Hebrew University there—particularly President Amnon Pazi, Rector Yoram Ben-Porath, Professor Shmuel Eisenstadt, and Ms. Liat Mayberg. The lectures I gave in Jerusalem generated the first draft of this book. I have rarely lectured to so intensely involved or so informed an audience as assembled those December afternoons on Mount Scopus. Their comments and questions started me on the road to fruitful revision. I also wish gratefully to acknowledge a grant from the Spencer Foundation that supported the work on which this volume is based.

At last I am able to express my gratitude to my publisher, Arthur Rosenthal, who, over the years, has censored any mention of his name from prefaces by me and other grateful authors. It is finally possible to escape his blue pencil, for he is now about to leave the directorship of Harvard University Press to preside over other matters elsewhere. Arthur Rosenthal as a publisher is a reward for hard work, a way of life. And as if that were not enough, there was the Press in its other embodiments: Angela von der Lippe, always skillfully encouraging, and Camille Smith, a manuscript editor with patience and imagination.

I have dedicated this book to Carol Fleisher Feldman, my wife and colleague. It will come as no surprise to anyone.

Acts of Meaning

CHAPTER ONE

The Proper Study of Man

I WANT TO BEGIN with the Cognitive Revolution as my point of departure. That revolution was intended to bring "mind" back into the human sciences after a long cold winter of objectivism. But mine will not be the usual account of progress marching ever forward.[1] For, at least in my view, that revolution has now been diverted into issues that are marginal to the impulse that brought it into being. Indeed, it has been technicalized in a manner that even undermines that original impulse. This is not to say that it has failed: far from it, for cognitive science must surely be among the leading growth shares on the academic bourse. It may rather be that it has become diverted by success, a success whose technological virtuosity has cost dear. Some critics, perhaps unkindly, even argue that the new cognitive science, the child of the revolution, has gained its technical successes at the price of dehumanizing the very concept of mind it had sought to reestablish in psychology, and that it has thereby estranged much of psychology from the other human sciences and the humanities.[2]

I shall have more to say on these matters shortly. But before going on, let me give you the plan of this chapter and the ones that follow. Once our retrospective glance at the revolution is done, I then want to turn directly to a preliminary exploration of a renewed cognitive revolution—a more interpretive approach to cognition concerned with "meaning-making," one that has been proliferating these last several years in anthropology, linguistics, philosophy, literary theory, psychology, and, it would almost seem, wherever one looks these days.[3] I rather suspect that this vigorous growth is an effort to recapture the original momentum of the first cognitive revolution. In later chapters, I shall try to fill in this preliminary sketch with some concrete illustration of research on the boundaries between psychology and its neighbors in the humanities and the social sciences, research that recaptures what I have called the originating impulse of the cognitive revolution.

Now let me tell you first what I and my friends thought the revolution was about back there in the late 1950s. It was, we thought, an all-out effort to establish meaning as the central concept of psychology—not stimuli and responses, not overtly observable behavior, not biological drives and their transformation, but meaning. It was *not* a revolution against behaviorism with the aim of transforming behaviorism into a better way of pursuing psychology by adding a little mentalism to it. Edward Tolman had done that, to little avail.[4] It was an altogether more profound revolution than that. Its aim was to discover and to describe formally the meanings that human beings created out of their encounters with the world, and then to propose hypotheses about what meaning-making processes were implicated. It focused upon the symbolic activities that human beings employed in constructing and in making sense not only of the world, but of themselves. Its aim was to prompt psychology to join forces with its sister interpretive disciplines in the humanities and in the social sciences. Indeed, beneath the surface of the more computationally oriented cognitive science, this is precisely what has been happening—first slowly and now with increasing momentum. And so today one finds flourishing centers of cultural psychology, cognitive and interpretive anthropology, cognitive linguistics, and above all, a thriving worldwide enterprise that occupies itself as never before since Kant with the philosophy of mind and of language. It is probably a sign of the times that the two Jerusalem-Harvard Lecturers in the academic year 1989–90 represent, each in his own way, this very tradition—Professor Geertz in anthropology and myself in psychology.

The cognitive revolution as originally conceived virtually required that psychology join forces with anthropology and linguistics, philosophy and history, even with the discipline of law. It is no surprise and certainly not an accident that in those early years the advisory board of the Center for Cognitive Studies at Harvard included a philosopher, W. V. Quine, an intellectual historian, H. Stuart Hughes, and a linguist, Roman Jakobson. Or that among the Center's Fellows could be numbered almost as many philosophers, anthropologists, and linguists as there were proper psychologists—among them such exponents of the new constructivism as Nelson Goodman. As for the law, I must report that several distinguished members of that faculty came occasionally to our colloquia. One of them, Paul Freund, admitted he came because we at the Center, it seemed to him, were interested in how rules (like rules of grammar, rather than scientific laws) affected human action and that, after all, is what jurisprudence is about.[5]

I think it should be clear to you by now that we were not out to "reform" behaviorism, but to replace it. As my colleague George Miller put it some years later, "We nailed our new credo to the door, and waited to see what would happen. All went very well, so well, in fact, that in the end we may have been the victims of our success."[6]

It would make an absorbing essay in the intellectual history of the last quarter-century to trace what happened to the originating impulse of the cognitive revolution, how it became fractionated and technicalized. The full story had best be left to the intellectual historians. All we need note now are a few signposts along the way, just enough of them to give a sense of the intellectual terrain on which we were all marching. Very early on, for example, emphasis began shifting from "meaning" to "information," from the *construction* of meaning to the *processing* of information. These are profoundly different matters. The key factor in the shift was the introduction of computation as the ruling metaphor and of computability as a necessary criterion of a good theoretical model. Information is indifferent with respect to meaning. In computational terms, information comprises an already precoded message in the system. Meaning is preassigned to messages. It is not an outcome of computation nor is it relevant to computation save in the arbitrary sense of assignment.

Information processing inscribes messages at or fetches them from an address in memory on instructions from a central control unit, or it holds them temporarily in a buffer store, and then manipulates them in prescribed ways: it lists, orders, combines, compares precoded information. The system that does all of these things is blind with respect to whether what is stored is words from Shakespeare's sonnets or numbers from a random number table. According to classic information theory, a message is informative if it reduces alternative choices.

This implies a code of established possible choices. The categories of possibility and the instances they comprise are processed according to the "syntax" of the system, its possible moves. Insofar as information in this dispensation can deal with meaning it is in the dictionary sense only: accessing stored lexical information according to a coded address. There are other "meaning-like" operations such as permuting a set of entries in order to test the resultants against a criterion, as in anagrams or Scrabble. But information processing cannot deal with anything beyond well-defined and arbitrary entries that can enter into specific relationships that are strictly governed by a program of elementary operations. Such a system cannot cope with vagueness, with polysemy, with metaphoric or connotative connections. When it seems to be doing so, it is a monkey in the British Museum, beating out the problem by a bone-crushing algorithm or taking a flyer on a risky heuristic. Information processing needs advance planning and precise rules.[7] It precludes such ill-formed questions as "How is the world organized in the mind of a Muslim fundamentalist?" or "How does the concept of Self differ in Homeric Greece and in the postindustrial world?" And it favors questions like "What is the optimum strategy for providing control information to an operator to ensure that a vehicle will be kept in a predetermined orbit?" We shall have much more to say later about meaning and the processes that create it. They are surprisingly remote from what is conventionally called "information processing."

It is not surprising, given that an Information Revolution was occurring throughout the postindustrial world, that such an emphasis should have developed. Psychology and the social sciences generally have always been sensitive, often oversensitive, to the needs of the society that gives them shelter. And it has always been rather an intellectual reflex of academic psychology to redefine man and his mind in the light of new social requirements. Nor is it surprising that under such conditions interest should have shifted away, accordingly, from mind and meaning to computers and information. For computers and computational theory had by the early 1950s become the root metaphor for information processing. Given preestablished meaning categories well-formed enough within a domain to provide a basis for an operating code, a properly programmed computer could perform prodigies of information processing with a minimum set of operations, and that is technological heaven. Very soon, computing became the model of the mind, and in place of the concept of meaning there emerged the concept of computability. Cognitive processes were equated with the programs that could be run on a computational device, and the success of one's effort to "understand," say, memory or concept attainment, was one's ability realistically to simulate such human conceptualizing or human memorizing with a computer program.[8] This line of thinking was enormously aided by Turing's revolutionary insight that any computational program, no matter how complex, could be "imitated" by a much simpler Universal Turing Machine computing with a finite set of quite primitive operations. If one falls into the habit of thinking of those complex programs as "virtual minds" (to borrow Daniel Dennett's phrase), then it takes only a small but crucial step to go the whole way to believing that "real minds" and their processes, like "virtual" ones and theirs, could be "explained" in the same way.[9]

This new reductionism provided an astonishingly libertarian program for the new cognitive science that was being born. It was so permissive, indeed, that even the old S-R learning theorist and associationist student of memory could come right back into the fold of the cognitive revolution so long as they wrapped their old concepts in the new terms of information processing. One did not have to truck with "mental" processes or with meaning at all. In place of stimuli and responses, there was input and output, with reinforcement laundered of its affective taint by being converted into a control element that fed information about the outcome of an operation back into the system. So long as there was a computable program, there was "mind."

At first this pun version of mind did not seem to provoke the traditional antimentalist panic among the seemingly converted behaviorists. In good time, though, new versions of old classically familiar controversies began to reemerge, particularly in connection with debates about the so-called architecture of cognition: whether it was to be conceived as a set of grammar-like hierarchically nesting rule structures for accepting, rejecting, or combining input, or whether, rather, it could be conceived of as a bottom-up connectionist network with completely distributed control as in the PDP (Parallel Distributed Processing) models, a model much like the old associationist doctrine, minus Herbart's creative synthesis. The first simulated the top-down, rationalist-mentalist tradition in psychology and moved easily back and forth between "real" minds and "virtual" ones; the second was a new version of what Gordon Allport used to mock in his lectures as "dustbowl empiricism." East Coast computationalism dealt with such mindlike terms as rules, grammars, and the like. The West Coasters wanted no part of such simulated mentalism.

Soon, the battleground began looking increasingly traditional and familiar, though the vehicles that were racing over it had much more speed and much more formalistic horsepower. But whether their maneuvers had to do with the *mind* or only with the theory of computation remained a question that both sides regarded as infinitely postponable. Time would tell, the questioners were assured, whether a sow's ear could be turned into a silk purse.[10]

It was inevitable that with computation as the metaphor of the new cognitive science and with computability as the necessary if not sufficient criterion of a workable theory within the new science, the old malaise about mentalism would re-emerge. With mind equated to program, what should the status of mental states be—old-fashioned mental states identifiable not by their programmatic characteristics in a computational system but by their subjective marking? There could be no place for "mind" in such a system—"mind" in the sense of intentional states like believing, desiring, intending, grasping a meaning. The cry soon rose to ban such intentional states from the new science. And surely no book published even in the heyday of early behaviorism could match the antimentalist zeal of Stephen Stich's *From Folk Psychology to Cognitive Science*.[11] There were, to be sure, statesmanlike efforts to make peace between the fuddy-duddy, mentalistic cognitivists and the brave new antimentalists. But they all took the form of either humoring or cajoling the mentalists. Dennett proposed, for example, that we should simply act *as if* people had intentional states that caused them to behave in certain ways; later we'd find out we didn't need such fuzzy notions.[12] Paul Churchland grudgingly admitted that, while it was interestingly problematic why people hung on so tenaciously to their plainly wrong mentalism, that was something to be explained rather than taken for granted. Perhaps, as Churchland put it, folk psychology seems to describe how things actually go, but how could a belief, desire, or attitude be a *cause* of anything in the physical world—that is, in the world of computation?[13] Mind in the subjective sense was either an epiphenomenon that the computational system outputted under certain conditions, in which case it could not be a cause of anything, or it was just a way that people talked about behavior after it had occurred (also an output), in which case it was just more behavior and simply needed further linguistic analysis. And yes, I must include Jerry Fodor's nativism: it could also be a spinoff of innate processes built into the system, in which case it was an effect rather than a cause.[14]

With the new attack on mental states and intentionality came a related attack on the concept of agency. Cognitive scientists, in the main, have no quarrel with the idea that behavior is directed, even directed toward goals. If direction is governed by the results of computing the utility of alternative outcomes, this is perfectly bearable and, indeed, it is the centerpiece of "rational choice theory." But cognitive science in its new mood, despite all its hospitality toward goal-directed behavior, is still chary of a concept of agency. For "agency" implies the conduct of action under the sway of intentional states. So action based on belief, desire, and moral commitment—unless it is purely stipulative in Dennett's sense—is now regarded as something to be eschewed by right-minded cognitive scientists. It is like free will among the determinists.[15] There were brave holdouts against the new anti-intentionalism, like the philosophers John Searle and Charles Taylor, or the psychologist Kenneth Gergen, or the anthropologist Clifford Geertz, but their views were marginalized by the majoritarians of mainstream computationalism.[16]

I am fully aware that I may be giving an exaggerated picture of what happened to the cognitive revolution once it became subordinated to the ideal of computability in the edifice of cognitive science. I note that whenever a proper cognitive scientist uses the expression "artificial intelligence" (even if it is only once), it is almost invariably followed by the capitalized initials "AI" in parentheses: "(AI)." I take this act of abbreviation to indicate one of two things. The abbreviated form suggests the shortening required by Zipf's Law: the length of a word or expression is inverse to its frequency—"television" eventually reduced to "TV"—with the abbreviation "(AI)" celebrating its comparable ubiquitousness and market penetration. The boast of AI is that it is about *all* mindlike artifacts, even about mind itself, if mind only be considered as yet another artifact, one that conforms to principles of computation. Or the abbreviation, on the other hand, may be a sign of embarrassment: either because there is an aura of obscenity about the artificialization of something so natural as intelligence (in Ireland, by the way, AI is the embarrassed abbreviation for artificial insemination), or because AI is an abbreviation of what, in its full form, might seem an oxymoron (the liveliness of intelligence coupled with the flatness of artificiality). The implied boast of Zipf's Law and the embarrassment of cover-up are both merited. There is no question that cognitive science has made a contribution to our understanding of how information is moved about and processed. Nor can there be much doubt on reflection that it has left largely unexplained and even somewhat obscured the very large issues that inspired the cognitive revolution in the first place. So let us return to the question of how to construct a mental science around the concept of meaning and the processes by which meanings are created and negotiated within a community.

II   Begin with the concept of culture itself—particularly its constitutive role. What was obvious from the start was perhaps too obvious to be fully appreciated, at least by us psychologists who by habit and by tradition think in rather individualistic terms. The symbolic systems that individuals used in constructing meaning were systems that were already in place, already "there," deeply entrenched in culture and language. They constituted a very special kind of communal tool kit whose tools, once used, made the user a reflection of the community. We psychologists concentrated on how individuals "acquired" these systems, how they made them their own, much as we would ask how organisms in general acquired skilled adaptations to the natural environment. We even became interested (again in an individualistic way) in man's specific innate readiness for language. But with a few exceptions, notably Vygotsky, we did not pursue the impact of language use on the nature of man as a species.[17] We were slow to grasp fully what the emergence of culture meant for human adaptation and for human functioning. It was not just the increased size and power of the human brain, not just bipedalism and its freeing of the hands. These were merely morphological steps in evolution that would not have mattered save for the concurrent emergence of shared symbolic systems, of traditionalized ways of living and working together—in short, of human culture.

The divide in human evolution was crossed when culture

became the major factor in giving form to the minds of those living under its sway. A product of history rather than of nature, culture now became the world to which we had to adapt and the tool kit for doing so. Once the divide was crossed, it was no longer a question of a "natural" mind simply *acquiring* language as an additive. Nor was it a question of a culture tuning or modulating biological needs. As Clifford Geertz puts it, without the *constituting* role of culture we are "unworkable monstrosities . . . incomplete or unfinished animals who complete or finish ourselves through culture."[18]

These are all by now rather banal conclusions in anthropology, but not in psychology. There are three good reasons to mention them here at the very start of our discussion. The first is a deep methodological point: the constitutive argument. It is man's participation *in* culture and the realization of his mental powers *through* culture that make it impossible to construct a human psychology on the basis of the individual alone. As my colleague of many years ago Clyde Kluckhohn used to insist, human beings do not terminate at their own skins; they are expressions of a culture. To treat the world as an indifferent flow of information to be processed by individuals each on his or her own terms is to lose sight of how individuals are formed and how they function. Or to quote Geertz again, "there is no such thing as human nature independent of culture."[19]

The second reason follows from this and is no less compelling. Given that psychology is so immersed in culture, it must be organized around those meaning-making and meaning-using processes that connect man to culture. This does *not* commit us to more subjectivity in psychology; it is just the reverse. By virtue of participation in culture, meaning is rendered *public* and *shared*. Our culturally adapted way of life depends upon shared meanings and shared concepts and depends as well upon shared modes of discourse for negotiating differences in meaning and interpretation. As I shall try to relate in the third chapter, the child does not enter the life of his or her group as a private and autistic sport of primary processes, but rather as a participant in a larger public process in which public meanings are negotiated. And in this process, meanings are not to his own advantage unless he can get them shared by others. Even such seemingly private phenomena as "secrets" (itself a culturally defined category) turn out once revealed to be publicly interpretable and even banal—just as patterned as matters openly admitted. There are even standardized means for "making excuses" for our exceptionality when the intended meanings of our acts become unclear, standard ways of making meaning public and thereby relegitimizing what we are up to.[20] However ambiguous or polysemous our discourse may be, we are still able to bring our meanings into the public domain and negotiate them there. That is to say, we live publicly by public meanings and by shared procedures of interpretation and negotiation. Interpretation, however "thick" it may become, must be publicly accessible or the culture falls into disarray and its individual members with it.

The third reason why culture must be a central concept for psychology lies in the power of what I shall call "folk psychology." Folk psychology, to which I shall devote the second chapter, is a culture's account of what makes human beings tick. It includes a theory of mind, one's own and others', a theory of motivation, and the rest. I should call it "ethnopsychology" to make the term parallel to such expressions as "ethnobotany," "ethnopharmacology," and those other naive disciplines that are eventually displaced by scientific knowledge. But folk psychology, though it changes, does not get displaced by scientific paradigms. For it deals with the nature, causes, and consequences of those intentional states—beliefs, desires, intentions, commitments—that most scientific psychology dismisses in its effort to explain human action from a point of view that is outside human subjectivity, formulated in Thomas Nagel's deft phrase as a "view from nowhere."[21] So folk psychology continues to dominate the transactions of everyday life. And though it changes, it resists being tamed into objectivity. For it is rooted in a language and a shared conceptual structure that are steeped in intentional states—in beliefs, desires, and commitments. And because it is a reflection of culture, it partakes in the culture's way of valuing as well as its way of knowing. In fact, it *must* do so, for the culture's normatively oriented institutions—its laws, its educational institutions, its family structures—serve to enforce folk psychology. Indeed, folk psychology in its turn serves to justify such enforcement. But that is a story for later.

Folk psychology is not once for all. It alters with the culture's changing responses to the world and to the people in it. It is worth asking how the views of such intellectual heroes as Darwin, Marx, and Freud gradually become transformed and absorbed into folk psychology, and I say this to make plain that (as we shall see in the final chapter) cultural psychology is often indistinguishable from cultural history.

Antimentalistic fury about folk psychology simply misses the point. The idea of jettisoning it in the interest of getting rid of mental states in our everyday explanations of human behavior is tantamount to throwing away the very phenomena that psychology needs to explain. It is in terms of folk-psychological categories that we experience ourselves and others. It is through folk psychology that people anticipate and judge one another, draw conclusions about the worth-whileness of their lives, and so on. Its power over human mental functioning and human life is that it provides the very means by which culture shapes human beings to its requirements. Scientific psychology, after all, is part of that same cultural process, and its stance toward folk psychology has consequences for the culture in which it exists—a matter to which we shall come presently.

III But I am going too far too fast, and riding roughshod over the cautions that most often make behavioral scientists shy away from a meaning-centered, culturally oriented psychology. These were the very cautions, I suspect, that made it easy for the Cognitive Revolution to shy away from some of its original aims. They are principally about two issues, both of them "founding issues" of scientific psychology. One concerns the restriction and sanitization of subjective states not so much as the *data* of psychology, for operationalism permits us to accept these as "discriminatory responses," for example, but as *explanatory* concepts. And certainly what I just proposed about the mediating role of meaning and culture and their embodiment in folk psychology seems to commit the "sin" of elevating subjectivity to an explanatory status. We psychologists were born in positivism and do not like such intentional-state notions as belief, desire, and intention as explanations. The other caution relates to relativism and the role of universals. A culturally based psychology sounds as if it must surely mire down into a relativism requiring a different

15

theory of psychology for each culture we study. Let me consider each of these cautions in turn.

Much of the distrust of subjectivism in our explanatory concepts has to do, I think, with the alleged discrepancy between what people *say* and what they actually *do*. A culturally sensitive psychology (especially one that gives a central role to folk psychology as a mediating factor) is and must be based not only upon what people actually *do*, but what they *say* they do and what they *say* caused them to do what they did. It is also concerned with what people *say* others did and why. And above all, it is concerned with what people *say* their worlds are like. Since the rejection of introspection as a core method of psychology, we have been taught to treat such "said" accounts as untrustworthy, even in some odd philosophical way as untrue. Our preoccupation with verificationist criteria of meaning, as Richard Rorty has pointed out, has made us devotees of prediction as the criterion of "good" science, including "good psychology."[22] Therefore, we judge what people say about themselves and their worlds or about others and theirs almost exclusively in terms of whether it predicts or provides a verifiable description of what they *do, did,* or *will do*. If it fails to do so, then with a Humean ferocity, we treat what was said as "naught but error and illusion." Or, perhaps, as merely "symptoms" that, when properly interpreted, will lead us to the true "cause" of the behavior whose prediction was our proper target.

Even Freud, with his sometime devotion to the idea of "psychic reality," fostered this cast of mind—since, as Paul Ricoeur so trenchantly puts it, Freud adhered at times to a nineteenth-century physicalist model that frowned on intentional-state explanations.[23] So it is part of our heritage as post-Freudian modern men and women to cock a snoot at what people *say*. It is "merely" manifest content. Real causes may not even be accessible to ordinary consciousness. We know all about ego defense and rationalization. As for knowledge of Self, it is a compromise symptom hardened in the interplay between inhibition and anxiety, a formation that, if it is to be known at all, must be archaeologically excavated with the tools of psychoanalysis.

Or in more contemporary terms, as in the careful studies reported by Lee Ross and Richard Nisbett, it is plain that people can describe correctly neither the basis of their choices nor the biases that skew the distribution of those choices.[24] And if even more powerful proof of this generalization were needed, it could be found in the work of Amos Tversky and Daniel Kahnemann who, indeed, cite as a precursor a well-known volume by Bruner, Goodnow, and Austin.[25]

There is a curious twist to the charge that "what people say is not necessarily what they do." It implies that what people *do* is more important, more "real," than what they *say,* or that the latter is important only for what it can reveal about the former. It is as if the psychologist wanted to wash his hands altogether of mental states and their organization, as if to assert that "saying," after all, is *only* about what one thinks, feels, believes, experiences. How curious that there are so few studies that go in the other direction: how does what one *does* reveal what one thinks or feels or believes? This in spite of the fact that our folk psychology is suggestively rich in such categories as "hypocrisy," "insincerity," and the like.

This one-sided emphasis of scientific psychology is indeed curious in light of our everyday ways of dealing with the relationship between saying and doing. To begin with, when

people act in an offensive fashion, our first step in coping is
to find out whether what they seem to have done is what
they really intended to do—to get some line on whether their
mental state (as revealed by saying) and their deed (as revealed
by doing) were in concordance or not. And if they say they
didn't intend to do it, we exonerate them. If they intended
their offensive act, we may then try to "reason with
them"—that is, to "talk them out of behaving in that way."
Or they may try to talk us out of our distaste for their action
by "giving an excuse," which is a verbal way of explicating
and thereby legitimizing their behavior as exempt from blame.
When people go on being offensive to a sufficiently large number of others, somebody may even try to convince them to go
to a psychiatrist who, through a *talking* cure, will try to get
their *behavior* straightened out.

Indeed, the meaning placed on most acts by the participants
in any everyday encounter depends upon what they say to one
another in advance, concurrently, or after they have acted. Or
what they are able to presuppose about what the other *would*
say, given a particular context. All of this is self-evident, not
only at the informal level of dialogue, but at the formal level
of privileged dialogue as codified, for example, in the legal
system. The law of contracts is entirely about the relationship
between performance and what was said. And so too, in a less
formal way, is the conduct of marriage, kinship, friendship,
and colleagueship.

It works in both directions. The meaning of talk is powerfully determined by the train of action in which it occurs—
"Smile when you say that!"—just as the meaning of action is
interpretable only by reference to what the actors say they are
up to—"So sorry" for an inadvertent bumping. After all, it

has now been a quarter-century since John Austin's introduction of speech act theory.[26] To those who want to concentrate upon whether what people say predicts what they will do, the only proper answer is that to separate the two in that way is to do bad philosophy, bad anthropology, bad psychology, and impossible law. Saying and doing represent a functionally inseparable unit in a culturally oriented psychology. When, in the next chapter, we come to discuss some of the "working maxims" of folk psychology, this will be a crucial consideration.

A culturally oriented psychology neither dismisses what people say about their mental states, nor treats their statements only as if they were predictive indices of overt behavior. What it takes as central, rather, is that the relationship between action and saying (or experiencing) is, *in the ordinary conduct of life,* interpretable. It takes the position that there is a publicly interpretable congruence between saying, doing, and the circumstances in which the saying and doing occur. That is to say, there are agreed-upon canonical relationships between the meaning of what we say and what we do in given circumstances, and such relationships govern how we conduct our lives with one another. There are procedures of negotiation, moreover, for getting back on the track when these canonical relations are violated. This is what makes interpretation and meaning central to a cultural psychology—or to any psychology or mental science, for that matter.

A cultural psychology, almost by definition, will not be preoccupied with "behavior" but with "action," its intentionally based counterpart, and more specifically, with *situated action*—action situated in a cultural setting, and in the mutually interacting intentional states of the participants. Which is not to say that a cultural psychology need dispense forevermore with laboratory experiments or with the search for human universals, a matter to which we turn now.

IV   I have urged that psychology stop trying to be "meaning free" in its system of explanation. The very people and cultures that are its subject are governed by shared meanings and values. People commit their lives to their pursuit and fulfillment, die for them. It has been argued that psychology must be culture-free if it is some day to discover a set of transcendent human universals—even if these universals are hedged by specifications about "cross-cultural" variations.[27] Let me propose a way of conceiving of human universals that is consistent with cultural psychology, yet escapes both the indeterminacies of relativism and the trivialities of cross-cultural psychology. Cultural psychology is *not* just a cross-cultural psychology that provides a few parameters to account for local variations in universal laws of behavior. Nor, as we shall see presently, does it condemn one to a rubbery relativism.

The solution to the issue of universals lies in exposing a widely held and rather old-fashioned fallacy that the human sciences inherited from the nineteenth century, a view about the relation between biology and culture. In that version, culture was conceived as an "overlay" on biologically determined human nature. The *causes* of human behavior were assumed to lie in that biological substrate. What I want to argue instead is that culture and the quest for meaning within culture are the proper causes of human action. The biological substrate, the so-called universals of human nature, is not a cause of action but, at most, a *constraint* upon it or a *condition* for it. The engine in the car does not "cause" us to drive to the supermarket for the week's shopping, any more than our biological reproductive system "causes" us with very high odds to marry somebody from our own social class, ethnic group, and so on. Granted that without engine-powered cars we would not drive to supermarkets, nor perhaps would there be marriage in the absence of a reproductive system.

But "constraint" puts the matter too negatively. For biologically imposed limits on human functioning are also challenges to cultural invention. The tool kit of any culture can be described as a set of prosthetic devices by which human beings can exceed or even redefine the "natural limits" of human functioning. Human tools are precisely of this order—soft ones and hard ones alike. There is, for example, a constraining biological limit on immediate memory—George Miller's famous "seven plus or minus two."[28] But we have constructed symbolic devices for exceeding this limit: coding systems like octal digits, mnemonic devices, language tricks. Recall that Miller's main point in that landmark paper was that by conversion of input through such coding systems we, as encultured human beings, are enabled to cope with seven *chunks* of information rather than with seven *bits*. Our knowledge, then, becomes encultured knowledge, indefinable save in a culturally based system of notation. In the process, we have broken through the original bounds set by the so-called biology of memory. Biology constrains, but not forevermore.

Or take the so-called natural human motives. It would be silly to deny that people get hungry or sexy or that there is a biological substrate for such states. But the devout Jew's commitment to fasting on Yom Kippur or the devout Muslim's commitment to Ramadan is not captured by a recital of the physiology of hunger. And the incest taboo is powerful and directive in a way that gonadotrophins are not. Nor is cultural commitment to certain foods or certain eating occasions simply a "conversion" of biological drives into psychological preferences. Our desires and our actions in their behalf are mediated by symbolic means. As Charles Taylor puts it in his brilliant new book, *Sources of the Self,* commitment is not just a preference. It is a belief, an "ontology" as he calls it, that a certain mode of life merits or deserves support, even though we find it difficult to live up to it. Our lives, as we shall see in the fourth chapter, are given over to finding such fulfillment as we can in terms of these ways of life—suffering to do so if necessary.

Obviously, there are also constraints on commitment to modes of life that are more biological than cultural. Physical exhaustion, hunger, sickness, and pain can break our connections or stem their growth. Elaine Scarry points out in her moving book *The Body in Pain* that the power of pain (as in torture) is that it obliterates our connection with the personal-cultural world and wipes out the meaningful context that gives direction to our hopes and strivings.[29] It narrows human consciousness to the point where, as torturers know, man literally becomes a beast. And even at that, pain does not always succeed, so powerful are the links to those meanings that give sense to life. The ghastly bestialization of the Holocaust and its death camps was designed as much to dehumanize as to kill, and it was this that made it the darkest moment in human history. Men have killed one another before, though never on such a scale or with such bureaucratization. But never has there been such a concerted effort to dehumanize through suffering, pain, and unbearable humiliation.

It was to the credit of Wilhelm Dilthey and his *Geisteswissenschaft*, his culturally based human science, that he recognized the power of culture to nurture and guide a new and ever-changing species.[30] I want to ally myself with his aspirations. What I want to argue in this book is that it is culture and the search for meaning that is the shaping hand, biology that is the constraint, and that, as we have seen, culture even has it in its power to loosen that constraint.

But lest this seem like a preface to a new optimism about humankind and its future, let me make one point before turning, as promised, to the issue of relativism. For all its generative inventiveness, human culture is not necessarily benign nor is it notably malleable in response to troubles. It is still customary, as in the fashion of ancient traditions, to lay the blame for the failings of human culture on "human nature"—whether as instincts, as original sin, or whatever. Even Freud, with his shrewd eye for human folly, often fell into this trap, notably in his doctrine of instinct. But this is surely a convenient and self-assuaging form of apologetics. Can we really invoke our biological heritage to account, say, for the invasive bureaucratization of life in our times, with its resultant erosion of selfhood and compassion? To invoke biological devils or the "Old Ned" is to dodge responsibility for what we ourselves have created. For all our power to construct symbolic cultures and to set in place the institutional forces needed for their execution, we do not seem very adept at steering our creations toward the ends we profess to desire. We do better to question our ingenuity in constructing and reconstructing communal ways of life than to invoke the failure of the human genome. Which is not to say that communal ways of life are easily changed, even in the absence of biological constraints, but only to focus attention where it belongs, not upon our biological limitations, but upon our cultural inventiveness.

V And this inevitably brings us to the issue of relativism. For what can we mean when we say that we are not very "adept" or "ingenious" in constructing our social worlds? Who judges so, and by what standards? If culture forms mind, and if minds make such value judgments, are we not locked into an inescapable relativism? We had better examine what this might mean. It is the epistemological side of relativism, rather than the evaluative, that must concern us first. Is what we know "absolute," or is it always relative to some perspective, some point of view? Is there an "aboriginal reality," or as Nelson Goodman would put it, is reality a construction?[31] Most thinking people today would opt for some mild perspectival position. But very few are prepared to abandon the notion of a singular aboriginal reality altogether. Indeed, Carol Feldman has even proposed a would-be human universal whose principal thesis is that we endow the conclusions of our cognitive reckonings with a special, "external" ontological status.[32] Our thoughts, so to speak, are "in here." Our conclusions are "out there." She calls this altogether human failing "ontic dumping," and she has never had to look far for instantiations of her universal. Yet, in most human interaction, "realities" are the results of prolonged and intricate processes of construction and negotiation deeply imbedded in the culture.

Are the consequences of practicing such constructivism and of recognizing that we do so as dire as they are made to seem? Does such a practice really lead to an "anything goes" relativism? Constructivism's basic claim is simply that knowledge is "right" or "wrong" in light of the perspective we have chosen to assume. Rights and wrongs of this kind—however well we can test them—do not sum to absolute truths and falsities. The best we can hope for is that we be aware of our own perspective and those of others when we make our claims of "rightness" and "wrongness." Put this way, constructivism hardly seems exotic at all. It is what legal scholars refer to as "the interpretive turn," or as one of them put it, a turning away from "authoritative meaning."

Richard Rorty, in his exploration of the consequences of pragmatism, argues that interpretivism is part of a deep, slow movement to strip philosophy of its "foundational" status.[33] He characterizes pragmatism—and the view that I have been expressing falls into that category—as "simply anti-essentialism applied to notions like 'truth,' 'knowledge,' 'language,' 'morality' and other similar objects of philosophical theorizing," and he illustrates it by reference to William James's definition of the "true" as "what is good in the way of belief." In support of James, Rorty remarks, "his point is that it is of no use being told that truth is 'correspondence with reality' . . . One can, to be sure, pair off bits of what one takes the world to be in such a way that the sentences one believes have internal structures isomorphic to relations between things in the world." But once one goes beyond such simple statements as "the cat is on the mat" and begins dealing with universals or hypotheticals or theories, such pairings become "messy and *ad hoc*." Such pairing exercises help very little in determining "why or whether our present view of the world is, roughly, the one we should hold." To push such an exercise to the limit, Rorty rightly insists, is "to want truth to have an essence," to be true in some absolute sense. But to say something useful about truth, he goes on, is to "explore practice rather than theory . . . action rather than contemplation." Abstract statements like "History is the story of the class struggle" are not to be judged by limiting oneself to questions like "Does that assertion get it right?" Pragmatic, perspectival questions would be more in order: "What would it be like to believe that?" or "What would I be committing myself to if I believed that?" And this is very far from the kind of Kantian essentialism that searches for principles that establish the defining essence of "knowledge" or "representation" or "rationality."[34]

Let me illustrate with a little case study. We want to know more about intellectual prowess. So we decide, unthinkingly, to use school performance as our measure for assessing "it" and predicting "its" development. After all, where intellectual prowess is concerned, school performance is of the essence. Then, in the light of our chosen perspective, Blacks in America have less "prowess" than Whites, who in their turn have slightly less than Asians. What kind of finding is *that*, asks the pragmatic critic? If goodwill prevails in the ensuing debate, a process of what can only be called deconstructing and reconstructing will occur. What does school performance mean, and how does it relate to other forms of performance? And about intellectual prowess, what does "it" mean? Is it singular or plural, and may not its very definition depend upon some subtle process by which a culture selects certain traits to honor, reward, and cultivate—as Howard Gardner has proposed?[35] Or, viewed politically, has school performance itself been rigged by choice of curriculum in such a way as to legitimize the offspring of the "haves" while marginalizing those of the "have nots"? Very soon, the issue of what "intellectual prowess" *is* will be replaced by questions of how we wish to *use* the concept in the light of a variety of circumstances—political, social, economic, even scientific.

That is a typical constructivist debate and a typical pragmatic procedure for resolving it. Is it relativism? Is it the dreaded form of relativism where every belief is as good as every other? Does anybody really hold such a view, or is relativism, rather, something conjured up by essentialist philosophers to shore up their faith in the "unvarnished truth"—an imaginary playmate forever assigned the role of spoiler in the game of pure reason? I think Rorty is right when he says that relativism is not the stumbling block for constructivism and pragmatism. Asking the pragmatist's questions—How does this view affect my view of the world or my commitments to it?—surely does not lead to "anything goes." It may lead to an unpacking of presuppositions, the better to explore one's commitments.

In his thoughtful book *The Predicament of Culture*, James Clifford notes that cultures, if they ever were homogeneous, are no longer so, and that the study of anthropology perforce becomes an instrument in the management of diversity.[36] It may even be the case that arguments from essences and from "aboriginal reality," by cloaking tradition with the mantle of "reality," are means for creating cultural stagnation and alienation. But what of the charge that constructivism weakens or undermines commitment?

If knowledge is relative to perspective, what now of the value issue, of one's *choice* of perspective? Is that "merely" a matter of preference? Are values only preferences? If not, how *do* we choose between values? There are two seductively misleading psychological views on this question—one of them seemingly rationalist in apparatus, the other romantically irrationalist. The latter holds that values are a function of gut reactions, displaced psychic conflicts, temperament, and the like. Insofar as the irrationalists take culture into account, it is as a source of supply, a cafeteria of values from which one chooses as a function of one's individual drives or conflicts. Values are not seen in terms of how they relate the individual to the culture, and their stability is accounted for by such fixatives as reinforcement schedules, neurotic rigidity, and so on.[37]

The rationalists take a quite different view, one derived principally from economic theory, best exemplified, perhaps, by rational choice theory.[38] According to rational choice theory, we express our values in our choices, situation by situation, guided by such rational models as utility theory, optimization rules, minimization of chagrin, or whatever. These choices (under appropriate conditions) reveal notable regularities, ones very reminiscent of the kinds of functions one observes in operant conditioning experiments with pigeons. But for a psychologist, the literature on "rational choice" is principally interesting for its vivid anomalies, its violations of the rules of utility. (Utility is the multiplicative resultant of the value of a particular choice and its subjective probability of being successfully executed, and it has been the cornerstone of formal economic theory since Adam Smith.) Consider the anomalies. Richard Herrnstein, for example, describes one amusingly called "dearer by the dozen" in which it can be shown that people prefer to buy season symphony tickets even when they know they will probably go to only half the concerts.[39] The way to handle the anomaly is to assign "snobbery" or "commitment" or "laziness" a value in the choice situation. The value assigned is one that makes the result conform to utility theory. And this, of course, gives the game away. If you accept utility theory (or one of its variants) you simply assign values to choices in a manner that makes choice behavior conform to its tenets. Rational choice theory has little or nothing to say about how values arise—whether they are gut reactions, whether historically determined, or what.

Both the irrationalist and the rationalist approaches to values miss one crucial point: values inhere in commitment to "ways of life," and ways of life in their complex interaction constitute a culture. We neither shoot our values from the hip, choice-situation by choice-situation, nor are they the product of isolated individuals with strong drives and compelling neuroses. Rather, they are communal and consequential in terms of our relations to a cultural community. They fulfill functions for us in that community. The values underlying a way of life, as Charles Taylor points out, are only lightly open to "radical reflection."[40] They become incorporated in one's self identity and, at the same time, they locate one in a culture. To the degree that a culture, in Sapir's sense, is not "spurious," the value commitments of its members provide either the basis for the satisfactory conduct of a way of life or, at least, a basis for negotiation.[41]

But the pluralism of modern life and the rapid changes it imposes, one can argue, create conflicts in commitment, conflicts in values, and therefore conflicts about the "rightness" of various claims to knowledge about values. We simply do not know how to predict the "future of commitment" under these circumstances. But it is whimsical to suppose that, under present world conditions, a dogged insistence upon the notion of "absolute value" will make the uncertainties go away. All one can hope for is a viable pluralism backed by a willingness to negotiate differences in world-view.

Which leads directly to one last general point I must make—one further reason why I believe that a cultural psychology such as I am proposing need not fret about the specter of relativism. It concerns open-mindedness—whether in politics, science, literature, philosophy, or the arts. I take open-mindedness to be a willingness to construe knowledge and values from multiple perspectives without loss of commitment to one's own values. Open-mindedness is the keystone of what we call a democratic culture. We have learned, with much pain, that democratic culture is neither divinely ordained nor is it to be taken for granted as perennially durable. Like all cultures, it is premised upon values that generate distinctive ways of life and corresponding conceptions of reality. Though it values the refreshments of surprise, it is not always proof against the shocks that open-mindedness sometimes inflicts. Its very open-mindedness generates its own enemies, for there is surely a biological constraint on appetites for novelty. I take the constructivism of cultural psychology to be a profound expression of democratic culture.[42] It demands that we be conscious of how we come to our knowledge and as conscious as we can be about the values that lead us to our perspectives. It asks that we be accountable for how and what we know. But it does not insist that there is only one way of constructing meaning, or one right way. It is based upon values that, I believe, fit it best to deal with the changes and disruptions that have become so much a feature of modern life.

VI Let me return finally to the adversarial stance of positivist "scientific psychology" toward "folk psychology." Scientific psychology insists quite properly upon its right to attack, debate, and even replace the tenets of folk psychology. It insists upon its right to deny the causal efficacy of mental states and of culture itself. At its furthest reach, indeed, it even assigns such concepts as "freedom" and "dignity" to the realm of illusion, though they are central to the belief system of a democratic culture. At this far reach, it is sometimes said of psychology that it is anticultural, antihistorical, and that its reductionism is anti-intellectual. Perhaps. But it is also true that the "village atheist" zeal of many extreme positivists has enlivened debates about the nature of man, and that their insistence on "objective" or "operational" research procedures has had a healthily astringent effect on our speculations. Yet there remains a niggling worry.

I recall the first of Wolfgang Kohler's William James Lectures at Harvard, *The Place of Values in a World of Facts*.[43] Kohler reports an imaginary conversation with a friend who complains of the "Nothing But" quality of psychology: that human nature is portrayed there as nothing but the concatenation of conditioned reflexes, associative bonds, transformed animal drives. And he worries, this imaginary friend, what happens when the postman and the prime minister also come to think this way. My worry too is what happens when the sitter comes to think he looks like his portrait. Remember Picasso's reply to Gertrude Stein's friends when they told him that she thought his portrait of her was not a good resemblance. "Tell her to wait," he said. "It will be." But the other possibility, of course, is that the sitter will become alienated from that kind of painter.[44] As Adrienne Rich puts it, "When someone with the authority of a teacher, say, describes the world and you are not in it, there is a moment of psychic disequilibrium, as if you looked into a mirror and saw nothing."[45]

Intellectuals in a democratic society constitute a community of cultural critics. Psychologists, alas, have rarely seen themselves that way, largely because they are so caught up in the self-image generated by positivist science. Psychology, on this view, deals only in objective truths and eschews cultural criticism. But even scientific psychology will fare better when it recognizes that its truths, like all truths about the human condition, are relative to the point of view that it takes toward that condition. And it will achieve a more effective stance toward the culture at large when it comes to recognize that the folk psychology of ordinary people is not *just* a set of self-assuaging illusions, but the culture's beliefs and working hypotheses about what makes it possible and fulfilling for people to live together, even with great personal sacrifice. It is where psychology starts and wherein it is inseparable from anthropology and the other cultural sciences. Folk psychology needs explaining, not explaining away.

CHAPTER TWO

Folk Psychology as an Instrument
of Culture

I N THE FIRST CHAPTER I recounted how the cognitive
revolution had been diverted from its originating impulse
by the computational metaphor, and I argued in favor of a
renewal and refreshment of the original revolution, a revolution inspired by the conviction that the central concept of a
human psychology is *meaning* and the processes and transactions involved in the construction of meanings.

This conviction is based upon two connected arguments.
The first is that to understand man you must understand how
his experiences and his acts are shaped by his intentional states,
and the second is that the form of these intentional states is
realized only through participation in the symbolic systems of
the culture. Indeed, the very shape of our lives—the rough
and perpetually changing draft of our autobiography that we
carry in our minds—is understandable to ourselves and to
others only by virtue of those cultural systems of interpretation. But culture is also constitutive of mind. By virtue of this
actualization in culture, meaning achieves a form that is public
and communal rather than private and autistic. Only by replac-
ing this transactional model of mind with an isolating individualistic one have Anglo-American philosophers been able to

make Other Minds seem so opaque and impenetrable. When we enter human life, it is as if we walk on stage into a play whose enactment is already in progress—a play whose somewhat open plot determines what parts we may play and toward what denouements we may be heading. Others on stage already have a sense of what the play is about, enough of a sense to make negotiation with a newcomer possible.

The view I am proposing reverses the traditional relation of biology and culture with respect to human nature. It is the character of man's biological inheritance, I asserted, that it does not direct or shape human action and experience, does not serve as the universal cause. Rather, it imposes constraints on action, constraints whose effects are modifiable. Cultures characteristically devise "prosthetic devices" that permit us to transcend "raw" biological limits—for example, the limits on memory capacity or the limits on our auditory range. The reverse view I am proposing is that it is culture, not biology, that shapes human life and the human mind, that gives meaning to action by situating its underlying intentional states in an interpretive system. It does this by imposing the patterns inherent in the culture's symbolic systems—its language and discourse modes, the forms of logical and narrative explication, and the patterns of mutually dependent communal life. Indeed, neuroscientists and physical anthopologists are coming increasingly to the view that cultural requirements and opportunities played a critical role in selecting neural characteristics in the evolution of man—a view most recently espoused by Gerald Edelman on neuroanatomical grounds, by Vernon Reynolds on the basis of physical anthropological evidence, and by Roger Lewin and Nicholas Humphrey with reference to primate evolutionary data.[1]

Those are the bare bones of the argument in favor of what I have called a "cultural" psychology—an effort to recapture not only the originating impulse of the Cognitive Revolution but also the program that Dilthey a century ago called the *Geisteswissenschaften,* the sciences of mental life.[2] In this chapter, we shall be principally concerned with one crucial feature of cultural psychology. I have called it "folk psychology," or you may prefer "folk social science" or even, simply, "common sense." All cultures have as one of their most powerful constitutive instruments a folk psychology, a set of more or less connected, more or less normative descriptions about how human beings "tick," what our own and other minds are like, what one can expect situated action to be like, what are possible modes of life, how one commits oneself to them, and so on. We learn our culture's folk psychology early, learn it as we learn to use the very language we acquire and to conduct the interpersonal transactions required in communal life.

Let me give you the bare bones of the argument I shall develop. I want first to explain what I mean by "folk psychology" as a system by which people organize their experience in, knowledge about, and transactions with the social world. I shall have to say a little about the history of the idea to make clearer its role in a cultural psychology. Then I shall turn to some of the crucial constituents of folk psychology, and that will eventually lead me to consider what kind of a cognitive system is a folk psychology. Since its organizing principle is narrative rather than conceptual, I shall have to consider the nature of narrative and how it is built around established or canonical expectations and the mental management of deviations from such expectations. Thus armed, we shall look more closely at how narrative organizes experience, using human

35

memory as our example. And finally, I shall want to explicate the "meaning-making" process in the light of the foregoing.

II   Coined in derision by the new cognitive scientists for its hospitality toward such intentional states as beliefs, desires, and meanings, the expression "folk psychology" could not be more appropriate for the uses to which I want to put it.[3] Let me sketch out its intellectual history briefly, for it will help put things in a broader context.

Its current usage began with a sophisticated revival of interest in "the savage mind" and particularly with the structure of indigenous classification systems. C. O. Frake published a celebrated study of the system for classifying skin diseases among the Subanun of Mindanao, and there followed detailed studies by others on ethnobotany, ethnonavigation, and the like. The ethnonavigation study detailed how Marshall Islanders navigated their outrigger sailing canoes to and from the Puluwat Atoll across bodies of open water by the use of stars, surface water signs, floating plants, chip logs, and odd forms of divination. It looked at navigation as seen and understood by a Puluwat navigator.[4]

But even before the prefix *ethno-* was affixed to these efforts, anthropologists had been interested in the underlying organization of experience among nonliterate people—why some peoples, such as the Talensee studied by Meyer Fortes in the 1930s, had no time-bound crisis definitions. Things happened when they were "ready." And there were even earlier studies: Margaret Mead's, for example, raising such questions as why life stages such as adolescence were so differently defined among the Samoans.[5]

Since, in the main, anthropologists had never been much smitten (with a few conspicuous exceptions) by the ideal of an objective, positivist science, they soon enough were led to the question of whether the shape of consciousness and experience of people in different cultures differed to a degree and in a manner that created a major problem of translation. Could one render the experience of the Puluwat navigator into the language and thought of the Western anthropologist—or that of the Western anthropologist into that of the Nilotic Nuer whose religion Edward Evans-Pritchard had studied? (When Evans-Pritchard had finished interviewing his informants about their religious beliefs, he courteously asked them whether they would like to ask him any questions about his. One of them asked shyly about the divinity that he wore on his wrist, consulted each time he seemed to make a major decision. Evans-Pritchard, a devout Catholic, was as surprised by the difficulty he had in explaining to his interlocutors that his wristwatch was not a deity as he was by the question they had asked in the first instance.)[6]

Somewhat later, a group of young sociologists led by Harold Garfinkel, mindful of the sorts of problems in epistemology such issues raised, took the radical step of proposing that in place of the classic sociological method—positing social classes, roles, and so on *ex hypothesi*—the social sciences might proceed by the rules of "ethnomethodology," creating a social science by reference to the social and political and human distinctions that people under study made in their everyday lives. In effect, Garfinkel and his colleagues were proposing an ethnosociology. And at about the same time, the psychologist Fritz Heider began arguing persuasively that, since human beings reacted to one another in terms of their *own* psychology (rather than, so to speak, the *psychologist's* psychology), we might do better to study the nature and origins of the "naive" psychology that gave meaning to their experience. In fact, neither Garfinkel's nor Heider's proposals were all that new. Garfinkel gave credit to the distinguished economist-sociologist Alfred Schutz, whose systematic writings, inspired by Continental phenomenology, had foreshadowed both Garfinkel's and Heider's programs as an antipositivist reform of the human sciences.[7]

There is a powerful *institutional* argument in the Schutzian claim—if I may so label the position we are considering. It is that cultural institutions are constructed in a manner to reflect commonsense beliefs about human behavior. However much the village atheism of a B. F. Skinner attempts to explain away human freedom and dignity, there remains the reality of the law of torts, the principle of contracts freely agreed to, and the obdurate solidity of jails, courthouses, property markers, and the rest. Stich (perhaps the most radical critic of folk psychology) chides Skinner for trying to "explain" such commonsense terms as desire, intention, and belief: they should, he insists, simply be ignored and not divert us from the grander task of establishing a psychology without intentional states.[8] But to ignore the institutionalized meanings attributed to human acts is about as effective as ignoring the state trooper who stands coolly by our car window and informs us that we have been traveling recklessly at ninety miles an hour and asks to see our license. "Reckless," "license," "state trooper"—all derive from the institutional matrix that society constructs to enforce a particular version of what constitutes reality. They are cultural meanings that guide and control our individual acts.

III   Since I am proposing that a folk psychology must be at the base of any cultural psychology, let me as a "participant observer" sample some major constituents of our own folk psychology to illustrate what I have in mind. These are, please note, simply *constituents*: that is to say, they are the elementary beliefs or premises that enter into the narratives about human plights of which folk psychology consists. An obvious premise of our folk psychology, for example, is that people have beliefs and desires: we *believe* that the world is organized in certain ways, that we *want* certain things, that some things *matter* more than others, and so on. We believe (or "know") that people hold beliefs not only about the present but about the past and future, beliefs that relate us to time conceived of in a particular way—our way, not the way of Fortes's Talensee or Mead's Samoans. We believe, moreover, that our beliefs should cohere in some way, that people should not believe (or want) seemingly irreconcilable things, although the principle of coherence is slightly fuzzy. Indeed, we also believe that people's beliefs and desires become sufficiently coherent and well organized as to merit being called "commitments" or "ways of life," and such coherences are seen as "dispositions" that characterize persons: loyal wife, devoted father, faithful friend. Personhood is itself a constituent concept of our folk psychology, and as Charles Taylor notes, it is attributed selectively, often withheld from those in an outgroup.[9] Note that it is only when constituent beliefs in a folk psychology are violated that narratives are constructed—a point about which I shall have much more to say presently. I mention it here to alert the reader to the canonical status of folk psychology: that it summarizes not simply how things are but (often implicitly)

39

how they should be. When things "are as they should be," the narratives of folk psychology are unnecessary.

Folk psychology also posits a world outside ourselves that modifies the expression of our desires and beliefs. This world is the context in which our acts are situated, and states of the world may provide reasons for our desires and beliefs—like Hillary climbing Everest because it was there, to take an extreme instance of supply creating demand. But we also know that desires may lead us to find meanings in contexts where others might not. It is idiosyncratic but explicable that some people like to cross the Sahara on foot or the Atlantic in a small boat. This reciprocal relation between perceived states of the world and one's desires, each affecting the other, creates a subtle dramatism about human action which also informs the narrative structure of folk psychology. When anybody is seen to believe or desire or act in a way that fails to take the state of the world into account, to commit a truly gratuitous act, he is judged to be folk-psychologically insane unless he as an agent can be narratively reconstrued as being in the grip of a mitigating quandary or of crushing circumstances. It may take a searching judicial trial in real life or a whole novel in fiction (as with André Gide's *Lafcadio's Adventure*) to effect such a reconstrual.[10] But folk psychology has room for such reconstruals: "truth is stranger than fiction." In folk psychology, then, people are assumed to have world knowledge that takes the form of beliefs, and are assumed to use that world knowledge in carrying out any program of desire or action.

The division between an "inner" world of experience and an "outer" one that is autonomous of experience creates three domains, each of which requires a different form of interpretation.[11] The first is a domain under the control of our own

40

intentional states: a domain where Self as agent operates with world knowledge and with desires that are expressed in a manner congruent with context and belief. The third class of events is produced "from outside" in a manner not under our own control. It is the domain of "nature." In the first domain we are in some manner "responsible" for the course of events; in the third not.

There is a second class of events that is problematic, comprising some indeterminate mix of the first and third, and it requires a more elaborate form of interpretation in order to allocate proper causal shares to individual agency and to "nature." If folk psychology embodies the interpretive principles of the first domain, and folk physics-cum-biology the third, then the second is ordinarily seen to be governed either by some form of magic or, in contemporary Western culture, by the scientism of physicalist, reductionist psychology or Artificial Intelligence. Among the Puluwat navigators, the introduction of a compass as a gift from the anthropologist (which they found interesting but which they rejected as superfluous) had them living briefly in the second domain.[12]

At their core, all folk psychologies contain a surprisingly complex notion of an agentive Self. A revealing but by no means atypical example is found among the Ilongot, a nonliterate people studied by Michelle and Renato Rosaldo. What makes for complexity is the shaping by culture of personal requirements—that fully agentive Ilongot male selfhood, for example, can be achieved only when an "enemy's" head is taken in an appropriate state of anger, or abstractly, that full selfhood involves the correct admixture of passion and knowledge. In one of the last papers she wrote before her untimely death working in the field, entitled "Toward an Anthropology of Self and Feeling," Michelle Rosaldo argues that notions like "self" or "affect" "grow not from 'inner' essence relatively independent of the social world, but from experience in a world of meanings, images, and social bonds, in which all persons are inevitably involved."[13]

In a particularly penetrating article on the American self, Hazel Markus and Paula Nurius propose that we think not of *a* Self but of Possible Selves along with a Now Self. "Possible selves represent individuals' ideas of what they *might* become, what they would *like* to become, and what they are *afraid* of becoming." Although not specifically intended to do so, their analysis highlights the extent to which American selfhood reflects the value placed in American culture on "keeping your options open." Contemporaneously, there began a trickle of clinical papers on the alarming rise of Multiple Personality Disorders as a principally American pathology, a gender-linked one at that. A recent review of the phenomenon by Nicholas Humphrey and Daniel Dennett even suggests that the pathology is engendered by therapists who accept the view that self is divisible and who, in the course of therapy, inadvertently offer this model of selfhood to their patients as a means of containing and alleviating their conflicts. Sigmund Freud himself remarked in "The Relation of the Poet to Daydreaming" that each of us is a cast of characters, but Freud had them locked within a single play or novel where, as an ensemble, they could enact the drama of neurosis on a single stage.[14]

I have given these two rather extended examples of the way Self is conceived in folk psychologies in two disparate cultures to reemphasize a critical point about the organizing principle of folk psychology as being narrative in nature rather than logical or categorical. Folk psychology is about human agents doing things on the basis of their beliefs and desires, striving for goals, meeting obstacles which they best or which best them, all of this extended over time. It is about Ilongot young men finding enough anger in themselves to take a head, and how they fare in that daunting effort; about young American women with conflicting and guilt-producing demands on their senses of identity finally resolving their dilemma (possibly with their doctors' unwitting help) by turning into an ego and an alter, and about the struggle to get the two back into communication.

IV   We must now concentrate more directly on narrative—what it is, how it differs from other forms of discourse and other modes of organizing experience, what functions it may serve, why it has such a grip on the human imagination. For we shall need to understand these matters better if we are to grasp the nature and power of folk psychology. Let me, then, in a preliminary way, set forth some of the properties of narrative.

Perhaps its principal property is its inherent sequentiality: a narrative is composed of a unique sequence of events, mental states, happenings involving human beings as characters or actors. These are its constituents. But these constituents do not, as it were, have a life or meaning of their own. Their meaning is given by their place in the overall configuration of the sequence as a whole—its plot or *fabula*. The act of grasping a narrative, then, is a dual one: the interpreter has to grasp the narrative's configuring plot in order to make sense of its constituents, which he must relate to that plot. But the plot configuration must itself be extracted from the succession of events. Paul Ricoeur, paraphrasing the British historian-philosopher W. B. Gallie, puts the matter succinctly:

> a story describes a sequence of actions and experiences of a certain number of characters, whether real or imaginary. These characters are represented in situations which change . . . [to] which they react. These changes, in turn, reveal hidden aspects of the situations and the characters, giving rise to a new predicament which calls for thought or action or both. The response to this predicament brings the story to its conclusion.[15]

I shall have much more to say later about these changes, predicaments, and the rest, but this will suffice for now.

A second feature of narrative is that it can be "real" or "imaginary" without loss of its power as a story. That is to say, the *sense* and the *reference* of story bear an anomalous relationship to each other. The story's indifference to extralinguistic reality underlines the fact that it has a structure that is internal to discourse. In other words, the sequence of its sentences, rather than the truth or falsity of any of those sentences, is what determines its overall configuration or plot. It is this unique sequentiality that is indispensable to a story's significance and to the mode of mental organization in terms of which it is grasped. Efforts to dethrone this "rule of sequence" as the hallmark of narrative have all yielded accounts of narrative that sacrifice its uniqueness to some other goal. Carl Hempel's celebrated essay "The Function of General Laws in History" is typical. By trying to "dechronologize" diachronic historical accounts into synchronic "social-science" propositions, Hempel succeeds only in losing particularity, in confusing interpretation and explanation, and in falsely relegating the narrator's rhetorical voice to the domain of "objectivity."[16]

The fact that the historian's "empirical" account and the novelist's imaginative story *share* the narrative form is, on reflection, rather startling. It has challenged thoughtful students both of imaginative literature and of history since Aristotle. Why the same form for fact and fiction? Does the first mimic the second or vice versa? How *does* narrative acquire its form? One answer, of course, is "tradition." And it is hard to deny that the forms of narrative are, as it were, sedimentary residues of traditional ways of telling, as with Albert Lord's thesis that all narrative is rooted in our ancient heritage of storytelling. In a related vein, Northrop Frye asserted that literature shapes itself out of its own traditions so that even its innovations grow out of traditional roots. Paul Ricoeur also sees tradition as providing what he calls "the impossible logic of narrative structures" through which myriad sequences are tied together to make narratives.[17]

But while convention and tradition surely play an important role in giving narrative its structures, I confess to a certain malaise with all thoroughgoing traditionalisms. Is it unreasonable to suppose that there is some human "readiness" for narrative that is responsible for conserving and elaborating such a tradition in the first place—whether, in Kantian terms, as "an art hidden in the human soul," whether as a feature of our language capacity, whether even as a psychological capacity like, say, our readiness to convert the world of visual input into figure and ground? By this I do not intend that we "store" specific archetypal stories or myths, as C. G. Jung has proposed.[18] That seems like misplaced concreteness. Rather, I mean a readiness or predisposition to organize experience into a narrative form, into plot structures and the rest. I shall set forth some evidence for such a hypothesis in the next chapter.

It seems to me that such a view is irresistible. And other scholars who have addressed the issue of narrative have been tempted along this path.

Most of the efforts to find such a "readiness" have been derived from Aristotle's notion of *mimesis*. Aristotle used the idea in the *Poetics* in order to describe the manner in which drama imitated "life," seeming to imply, thereby, that narrative, somehow, consisted of reporting things as they had happened, the order of narrative thus being determined by the order of events in a life. But a close reading of the *Poetics* suggests that he had something else in mind. *Mimesis* was the capturing of "life in action," an elaboration and amelioration of what happened. Even Paul Ricoeur, perhaps the deepest and most indefatigable modern student of narrative, has difficulties with the idea. Ricoeur likes to note the kinship between "being *in* history" and "telling *about* it," noting that the two have a certain "mutual belongingness." "The form of life to which narrative discourse belongs is our historical condition itself." Yet he too has trouble sustaining his figure of speech. "*Mimesis*," he tells us, "is a kind of metaphor of reality." "It refers to reality not in order to copy it, but in order to give it a new reading." It is by virtue of this metaphoric relationship, he then argues, that narrative can proceed even with "the suspension of the referential claim of ordinary language"—that is, without obligation to "match" a world of extralinguistic reality.[19]

If the mimetic function is interpretive of "life in action," then it is a very complex form of what C. S. Peirce long ago called an "interpretant," a symbolic schema for mediating between sign and "world"—an interpretant that exists at some higher level than the word or the sentence, in the realm of discourse itself.[20] We have still to consider where the capacity to create such complex symbolic interpretants comes from, if it is not merely art copying life. And that is what we shall have to concern ourselves with in the following chapter. But there are other matters that must engage us first.

V   Another crucial feature of narrative, as already noted in passing, is that it specializes in the forging of links between the exceptional and the ordinary. To this matter now. Let me begin with a seeming dilemma. Folk psychology is invested in canonicality. It focuses upon the expectable and/or the usual in the human condition. It endows these with legitimacy or authority.[21] Yet it has powerful means that are purpose-built for rendering the exceptional and the unusual into comprehensible form. For as I insisted in the opening chapter, the viability of a culture inheres in its capacity for resolving conflicts, for explicating differences and renegotiating communal meanings. The "negotiated meanings" discussed by social anthropologists or culture critics as essential to the conduct of a culture are made possible by narrative's apparatus for dealing simultaneously with canonicality and exceptionality. Thus, while a culture must contain a set of norms, it must also contain a set of interpretive procedures for rendering departures from those norms meaningful in terms of established patterns of belief. It is narrative and narrative interpretation upon which folk psychology depends for achieving this kind of meaning. Stories achieve their meanings by explicating deviations from the ordinary in a comprehensible form—by providing the "impossible logic" discussed in the preceding section. We had better examine this matter more closely now.

Begin with the "ordinary," what people take for granted about the behavior that is going on around them. In every culture, for example, we take for granted that people behave in a manner appropriate to the setting in which they find themselves. Indeed, Roger Barker dedicated twenty years of perceptive research to demonstrating the power of this seemingly banal social rule.[22] People are expected to behave situationally whatever their "roles," whether they are introverted or extraverted, whatever their scores on the MMPI, whatever their politics. As Barker put it, when people go into the post office, they behave "post-office."

The "situation rule" holds for speaking as well as for acting. Paul Grice's Cooperative Principle captures the idea well. Grice proposed four maxims about how conversational exchanges are and/or should be conducted—maxims of quality, quantity, and manner: our replies to one another should be brief, perspicuous, relevant, and truthful. Departures from these maxims create surplus meaning by producing what Grice calls "conversational implicatures," triggers that set off searches for a "meaning" in the exceptional, for meanings that inhere in the nature of their departure from ordinary usage.[23]

When people behave in accordance with Barker's principle of situatedness or with Grice's maxims of conversational exchange, we do not ask *why*: the behavior is simply taken for granted as in need of no further explanation. Because it is ordinary, it is experienced as canonical and therefore as self-explanatory. We take it for granted that if you ask somebody where R. H. Macy's is, they will give you relevant, correct, perspicuous, and brief directions; *that* kind of response requires no explanation. People will think it exceedingly odd if you do question *why* people are behaving in this way—"post-office" in the post office, and brief, perspicuous, relevant, and sincere in answering requests for directions. Pressed to come up with an account of what already seems self-explanatory, interlocutors will reply with either a quantifier ("Everybody does that") and/or a deontic modal ("That's what you're *supposed* to do"). The brunt of their explanation will be to indicate the appropriateness of the context as a location for the act in question.

In contrast, when you encounter an exception to the ordinary, and ask somebody what is happening, the person you ask will virtually always tell a story that contains *reasons* (or some other specification of an intentional state). The story, moreover, will almost invariably be an account of a possible world in which the encountered exception is somehow made to make sense or to have "meaning." If somebody comes into the post office, unfurls the Stars and Stripes, and commences to wave it, your folk-psychological interlocutor will tell you, in response to your puzzled question, that today is probably some national holiday that he himself had forgotten, that the local American Legion Post may be having a fundraiser, or even simply that the man with the flag is some kind of nationalistic nut whose imagination has been touched by something in this morning's tabloid.

All such stories seem to be designed to give the exceptional behavior meaning in a manner that implicates both an intentional state in the protagonist (a belief or desire) and some canonical element in the culture (national holiday, fundraiser, fringe nationalism). *The function of the story is to find an intentional state that mitigates or at least makes comprehensible a devia-*

49

tion from a canonical cultural pattern. It is this achievement that gives a story verisimilitude. It may also give it a peacekeeping function, but that matter can wait until a later chapter.

VI   Having considered three characteristics of narrative—its sequentiality, its factual "indifference," and its unique way of managing departures from the canonical—we must turn now to its dramatic quality. Kenneth Burke's classic discussion of "dramatism," as he called it nearly a half-century ago, still serves well as a starting point.[24] Well-formed stories, Burke proposed, are composed of a pentad of an Actor, an Action, a Goal, a Scene, and an Instrument—plus Trouble. Trouble consists of an imbalance between any of the five elements of the pentad: an Action toward a Goal is inappropriate in a particular Scene, as with Don Quixote's antic maneuvers in search of chivalric ends; an Actor does not fit the Scene, as with Portnoy in Jerusalem or Nora in *A Doll's House*; or there is a dual Scene as in spy thrillers, or a confusion of Goals as with Emma Bovary.

Dramatism, in Burke's sense, focuses upon deviations from the canonical that have moral consequences—deviations related to legitimacy, moral commitment, values. Stories must necessarily, then, relate to what is morally valued, morally appropriate, or morally uncertain. The very notion of Trouble presupposes that Actions should fit Goals appropriately, Scenes be suited to Instruments, and so on. Stories, carried to completion, are explorations in the limits of legitimacy, as Hayden White has pointed out.[25] They come out "lifelike," with a Trouble morally explicated if not redressed. And if imbalances hang ambiguously, as they often do in postmodern fiction, it is because narrators seek to subvert the conventional means through which stories take a moral stand. To tell a story is inescapably to take a moral stance, even if it is a moral stance against moral stances.

There is another feature of well-formed narrative, what I have called elsewhere its "dual landscape."[26] That is to say, events and actions in a putative "real world" occur concurrently with mental events in the consciousness of the protagonists. A discordant linkage between the two, like Trouble in the Burkean pentad, provides motive force to narrative—as with Pyramis and Thisbe, Romeo and Juliet, Oedipus and his wife/mother Jocasta. For stories have to do with how protagonists interpret things, what things mean to them. This is built into the circumstance of story—that it involves both a cultural convention and a deviation from it that is explicable in terms of an individual intentional state. This gives stories not only a moral status but an epistemic one.

Modernist literary narrative, to use Erich Kahler's phrase, has taken an "inward turn" by dethroning the omniscient narrator who knew both about the world "as it was" and about what his protagonists were making of it.[27] By getting rid of him, the modern novel has sharpened contemporary sensibility to the conflict inherent in two people trying to know the "outer" world from different perspectives. It is a point worth noting, for it illustrates the extent to which different historical cultures deal with the relation between the two "landscapes." Erich Auerbach, who traces the history of the representation of reality in Western literature in his *Mimesis*, begins with the narratorially certain realities of the *Odyssey* and ends with Virginia Woolf's attenuated phenomenology in *To the Lighthouse*.[28] It is worth more than a passing thought that from,

51

say, Flaubert and Conrad to the present, the Trouble that drives literary narrative has become, as it were, more epistemic, more caught up in the clash of alternative meanings, less involved in the settled realities of a landscape of action. And perhaps this is true of mundane narrative as well. In this respect, life must surely have imitated art by now.

It begins to be clear why narrative is such a natural vehicle for folk psychology. It deals (almost from the child's first talk, as we shall see in the next chapter) with the stuff of human action and human intentionality. It mediates between the canonical world of culture and the more idiosyncratic world of beliefs, desires, and hopes. It renders the exceptional comprehensible and keeps the uncanny at bay—save as the uncanny is needed as a trope. It reiterates the norms of the society without being didactic. And, as presently will be clear, it provides a basis for rhetoric without confrontation. It can even teach, conserve memory, or alter the past.

VII   I have said very little thus far about the structural kinship or the affinity between "fictional" and "empirical" narratives, a matter I raised earlier in considering the indifference of narrative with respect to reference. Given the specialization of ordinary languages in establishing binary contrasts, why do none of them impose a once-for-all, sharp grammatical or lexical distinction between true stories and imaginative ones? As if to mock the distinction, fiction often dresses itself in the "rhetoric of the real" to achieve its imaginative verisimilitude. And we know from studies of the autobiographical form particularly that fictional forms often provide the structural lines in terms of which "real lives" are organized. Indeed, most Western languages retain words in their lexicon that seem perversely to subvert the distinction between *Dichtung* and *Wahrheit*: *storia* in Italian, *histoire* in French, *story* in English. If truth and possibility are inextricable in narrative, this would put the narratives of folk psychology into a strange light, leaving the listener, as it were, bemused about what is of the world and what of the imagination. And, indeed, such is frequently the case: is a particular narrative explication simply a "good story," or is it the "real thing"? I want to pause briefly over this curious blurriness, for I think it reveals something important about folk psychology.

Go back to our earlier discussion of *mimesis*. Recall Ricoeur's claim that "story" (whether factual or imaginative) invites reconstrual of what might have happened. Wolfgang Iser makes the same point when he remarks that a characteristic of fiction is that it places events in a wider "horizon" of possibilities.[29] In *Actual Minds, Possible Worlds,* I tried to show how the language of skillful narrative differs from that of skillful exposition in its employment of "subjunctivizing transformations." These are lexical and grammatical usages that highlight subjective states, attenuating circumstances, alternative possibilities. A short story by James Joyce contrasted sharply with an exemplary ethnographic account by Martha Weigel of Penitente blood brotherhood not only in the authors' use of these "subjunctifiers" but also in the reader's incorporation of them in talking about what had been read. The "story" ended up in memory even more subjunctivized than it had been written; the "exposition" ended up there much as given in the text. To make a *story* good, it would seem, you must make it somewhat uncertain, somehow open to variant readings, rather subject to the vagaries of intentional states, undetermined.

A story that succeeds in achieving such requisite uncertainty or subjunctivity—that achieves what the Russian Formalist critics referred to as its "literariness," its *literaturnost*—must serve some rather special functions for those who fall under its sway. Unfortunately, we know very little about this matter, but I would like to offer some purely speculative hypotheses about it, if the skeptical reader will bear with me.

The first is that "subjunctive" stories are easier to enter into, easier to identify with. Such stories, as it were, can be tried on for psychological size, accepted if they fit, rejected if they pinch identity or compete with established commitments. The child's "omnipotence of thought," I suspect, remains sufficiently unwithered during adulthood for us to leap through the proscenium to become (if only for a moment) whoever may be on stage in whatever plight they may find themselves. Story, in a word, is vicarious experience, and the treasury of narratives into which we can enter includes, ambiguously, either "reports of real experience" or offerings of culturally shaped imagination.

The second hypothesis has to do with learning to distinguish, to use Yeats's phrase, "the dancer from the dance." A story is *somebody's* story. Despite past literary efforts to stylize the narrator into an "omniscient I," stories inevitably have a narratorial voice: events are seen through a particular set of personal prisms. And particularly when stories take the form, as they so often do (as we shall see in the following chapter), of justifications or "excuses," their rhetorical voice is plain. They do not have the "sudden death" quality of objectively framed expositions where things are portrayed as "as they are." When we want to bring an account of something into the domain of negotiated meanings, we say of it, ironically, that it was a "good story." Stories, then, are especially viable instruments for social negotiation. And their status, even when they are hawked as "true" stories, remains forever in the domain midway between the real and the imaginary. The perpetual revisionism of historians, the emergence of "docudramas," the literary invention of "faction," the pillow talk of parents trying to make revised sense of their children's doings—all of these bear testimony to this shadowy epistemology of the story. Indeed, the existence of story as a form is a perpetual guarantee that humankind will "go meta" on received versions of reality. May that not be why dictators must take such draconian measures against a culture's novelists?

And one last speculation. It is easier to live with alternative versions of a story than with alternative premises in a "scientific" account. I do not know in any deep psychological sense why this should be so, although I have a suspicion. We *know* from our own experience in telling consequential stories about *ourselves* that there is an ineluctably "human" side to making sense. And we are prepared to accept another version as "only human." The Enlightenment spirit that led Carl Hempel, mentioned earlier, to propose that history should be "reduced" to testable propositional forms, lost sight of the negotiatory and hermeneutic function of history.

VIII   I want to turn now to the role of narrativized folk psychology in what, broadly, might be called the "organization of experience." Two matters interest me particularly. One of them, rather traditional, is usually called *framing* or schematizing, the other is *affect regulation*. Framing provides a means of "constructing" a world, of characterizing its flow, of segmenting events within that world, and so on. If we were not able to do such framing, we would be lost in a murk of chaotic experience and probably would not have survived as a species in any case.

The typical form of framing experience (and our memory of it) is in narrative form, and Jean Mandler has done us the service of drawing together the evidence showing that what does *not* get structured narratively suffers loss in memory.[30] Framing pursues experience into memory, where, as we have known since the classic studies of Bartlett, it is systematically altered to conform to our canonical representations of the social world, or if it cannot be so altered, it is either forgotten or highlighted in its exceptionality.

This is all a familiar story, but it has been somewhat trivialized by being made to seem like a completely individual phenomenon—merely a matter of the laying down of traces and schemata within each individual brain, as it were. Bartlett, now long gone, has himself been recently accused by critics of having abandoned an initially "cultural" view of the framing of memory in favor of a more individualistic psychological one. The shift from a less well known article of 1923 to the renowned book of 1932 is discussed in an essay by John Shotter. Shotter insists very strongly that framing is *social*, designed for the *sharing* of memory within a culture rather than simply to ensure individual storage.[31] He cites the redoubtable social critic and anthropologist Mary Douglas as saying, "The author of the best book on remembering forgot his first convictions [and] became absorbed into the institutional framework of Cambridge University psychology, and restricted by the conditions of the experimental laboratory."[32]

But Bartlett surely did not forget the "cultural" part of what he had set out to explore. In a final section of his celebrated book, dealing with the "social psychology of remembering," he says:

> Every social group is organized and held together by some specific psychological tendency or group of tendencies, which give the group a bias in its dealings with external circumstances. The bias constructs the special persistent features of group culture . . . [and this] immediately settle[s] what the individual will observe in his environment and what he will connect from his past life with this direct response. It does this markedly in two ways. First, by providing that setting of interest, excitement, and emotion which favors the development of specific images, and secondly, by providing a persistent framework of institutions and customs which acts as a schematic basis for constructive memory.[33]

About the "schematizing" power of institutions to which he refers, let me restate a point I made earlier. Experience in and memory of the social world are powerfully structured not only by deeply internalized and narrativized conceptions of folk psychology but also by the historically rooted institutions that a culture elaborates to support and enforce them. Scott Fitzgerald was right when he said that the very rich are "different," and not just because they have fortunes: they are *seen* as different, and, indeed, act accordingly. Even "science" reinforces these perceptions and their memory transformations, as we know from such recent books as Cynthia Fuchs Epstein's *Deceptive Distinctions*, which demonstrates how gender stereotypes were systematically highlighted and exaggerated by the selective choice of research instruments to measure them.[34] The very structure of our lexicon, while it may not force us to code human events in a particular way, certainly predisposes us to be culturally canonical.

Now consider those culturally imposed ways of directing and regulating affect in the interest of cultural cohesion to which Bartlett refers. He insists in *Remembering* that what is most characteristic of "memory schemata" as he conceives them is that they are under the control of an affective "attitude." Indeed, he remarks that any "conflicting tendencies" likely to disrupt individual poise or to menace social life are likely to destabilize memory organization as well. It is as if unity of affect (in contrast to "conflict") is a condition for economical schematization of memory.

Indeed, Bartlett goes further than that. In the actual effort to remember something, he notes, what most often comes first to mind is an affect or a charged "attitude"—that "it" was something unpleasant, something that led to embarrassment, something that was exciting. The affect is rather like a general thumbprint of the schema to be reconstructed. "The recall is then a construction made largely on the basis of this attitude, and its general effect is that of a justification of the attitude." Remembering serves, on this view, to justify an affect, an attitude. The act of recall is "loaded," then, fulfilling a "rhetorical" function in the process of reconstructing the past. It is a reconstruction designed to justify. The rhetoric, as it were, even determines the form of "invention" we slip into in reconstructing the past: "The confident subject justifies himself—attains a rationalization, so to speak—by setting down more detail than was actually present; while the cautious, hesitating subject reacts in the opposite manner, and finds his justifica-

tion by diminishing rather than increasing the details presented [in the experiment]."[35]

But I would want to add an interpersonal or cultural dimension to Bartlett's account. We are not only trying to convince
ourselves with our memory reconstructions. Recalling the past
also serves a dialogic function. The rememberer's interlocutor
(whether present in the flesh or in the abstract form of a
reference group) exerts a subtle but steady pressure. That is
surely the brunt of Bartlett's own brilliant experiments on
serial reproduction, in which an initially culturally alien Amer-
indian tale comes out culturally conventionalized when passed
in succession from one Cambridge undergraduate to another.
In Bartlett's phrase, we create "sympathetic weather" in our
memory reconstructions. But it is sympathetic weather not
only for ourselves but for our interlocutors.

In a word, the very processes involved in "having and hold-
ing" experience are informed by schemata steeped in folk psychological conceptions of our world—the constituent beliefs
and the larger-scale narratives that contain them in those tem-
poral configurations or plots to which reference was made
earlier.

IX   But narrative is not just plot structure or dramatism.
Nor is it just "historicity" or diachronicity. It is also a way of
using language. For it seems to depend for its effectiveness,
as I have already noted in discussing its "subjunctivity," upon
its "literariness"—even in the recounting of everyday tales. To
a striking degree, it relies upon the power of tropes—upon
metaphor, metonymy, synecdoche, implicature, and the rest.
Without them it loses its power to "expand the horizon of

possibilities," to explore the full range of connections between the exceptional and the ordinary.[36] Indeed, recall that Ricoeur even speaks of *mimesis* as a "metaphor of reality."

Narrative, moreover, must be concrete: it must "ascend to the particular," as Karl Marx once put it.[37] Once it achieves its particularities, it converts them into tropes: its Agents, Actions, Scenes, Goals, and Instruments (and its Troubles as well) are converted into emblems. Schweitzer becomes "compassion," Talleyrand "shrewdness," Napoleon's Russian campaign the tragedy of overreached ambition, the Congress of Vienna an exercise in imperial wheeling and dealing.

There is one overriding property that all such "emblems" share that makes them different from logical propositions. Impenetrable to both inference and induction, they resist logical procedures for establishing what they *mean*. They must, as we say, be *interpreted*. Read three of Ibsen's plays: *The Wild Duck, A Doll's House,* and *Hedda Gabler.* There is no way of arriving logically at their "truth conditions." They cannot be decomposed into a set of atomic propositions that would allow the application of logical operations. Nor can their "gists" be extracted unambiguously. Is the returned son in *The Wild Duck* an emblem of envy, of idealism, or, as he hints darkly in his closing lines, does he stand for all those "destined to be the thirteenth guest at dinner"? Is Nora in *A Doll's House* a premature feminist, a frustrated narcissist, or a woman paying the high price for respectability? And Hedda: Is this a story about the spoiled child of a famous father, about the death implicit in the hope for perfection, about the inevitable complicity in self-deception? The interpretation we offer, whether historical or literary or judicial, is, as we have already noted, always normative. You cannot argue any of these interpretations without taking a moral stance and a rhetorical posture. Any more than you can univocally interpret the stories on both sides of a family quarrel or the "arguments" on both sides of a First Amendment case before the U.S. Supreme Court. Indeed, the very speech act implied in "telling a story"—whether from life or from the imagination—warns the beholder that its meaning cannot be established by Frege-Russell rules relating to sense and reference.[38] We interpret stories by their verisimilitude, their "truth likeness," or more accurately, their "lifelikeness."

Interpretive meanings of the kind we are considering are metaphoric, allusive, very sensitive to context. Yet they are the coin of culture and of its narrativized folk psychology. Meaning in this sense differs in some fundamental way from what philosophers in the dominant Anglo-American tradition have meant by "meaning." Does this imply that "cultural meaning" must be, therefore, a totally impressionistic or literary category? If this were so, then the portents would not be good for a cultural psychology that had the "looser" concept of meaning at its center. But I do not think this is so, and I must now explain.

At the beginning of this century, Anglo-American philosophy turned its back on what is traditionally called "psychologism." There must be no confusion between the *process* of thinking, on the one side, and "pure thought" on the other. The former is totally irrelevant to the realm of meaning in its philosophical sense: it is subjective, private, context-sensitive, and idiosyncratic, whereas pure thoughts, embodied in propositions, are shared, public, and amenable to rigorous scrutiny. Early Anglo-American philosophers (and I include Gottlob Frege among them, for he inspired the movement) looked with deep suspicion upon natural language, and chose to conduct their enterprise in the decontextualized medium of formal logic.[39] Nobody doubted that there was a genuine problem about how individual minds came to grasp idiosyncratic meanings, but that was not the central philosophical problem. The philosophical problem, rather, was to determine the meanings of sentences or propositions *as written*. This was to be done by establishing their reference and sense: reference by determining the conditions for a sentence's truth, sense by establishing what other sentences it might relate to. Truth was objective: sentences are true or false whether we recognize them as such or not. Sense in general was independent of any particular or private sense—a matter that was never fully developed, probably because it could not be. Under this dispensation, meaning became a philosopher's tool, a formal instrument of logical analysis.

Decontextualized sentences in the formal logical tradition are as if uttered from nowhere by nobody—texts on their own, "unsponsored."[40] Establishing the meaning of such texts involves a highly abstract set of formal operations. Many psychologists, linguists, anthropologists, and increasing numbers of philosophers complained that the dependence of meaning upon "verification" conditions left the broader, human concept of meaning as related to use virtually untouched.

Led by speech-act theorists inspired by John Austin directly and Wittgenstein indirectly, students of mind have centered their efforts during the last thirty years upon restoring the communicative context back into discussions of meaning.[41] While utterances were treated in the classical tradition as decontextualized or unsponsored locutions, they could also be treated in a principled way as expressing a speaker's communicative intention. And, in the same spirit, one could then inquire whether the speaker's meaning was grasped or "taken up" by a hearer and what determined that uptake. As we all know, uptake depends upon the speaker and listener's sharing a set of conventions for communicating different types of meaning. Nor were these meanings limited to matters of reference and truth.

Utterances embodied many more intentions than merely to refer: to request, to promise, to warn, and even, at times, to perform a ritual cultural function, as in the act of christening. The shared conventions that fitted a speaker's utterance to the occasions of its use were not truth conditions but *felicity conditions*: rules not only about the propositional content of an utterance but about required contextual preconditions, about sincerity in the transaction, and about essential conditions defining the nature of the speech act (for example, to "promise" you must be able to deliver). Later, Paul Grice enriched the account by noting that all of these conventions were further constrained by the Cooperative Principle to which I alluded earlier—a set of maxims about the brevity, relevance, perspicuousness, and sincerity of conversational exchanges.[42] And from this grew the powerful idea that meaning is also generated by the breaching of these maxims in conventionalized ways.

With the introduction of felicity conditions and the Gricean maxims, the "unsponsored text" on the logician's blackboard made place for situated speech bearing the illocutionary force of an utterer's intent. Meaning in situated speech became cultural and conventional. And its analysis became empirically based and principled rather than merely intuitive. It is in this spirit that I have proposed the restoration of meaning-making as the central process of a cultural psychology, of a refreshed Cognitive Revolution. I think the concept of "meaning" understood in this principled way has reconnected linguistic conventions with the web of conventions that constitute a culture.

One last word about meaning, particularly as it may be contingent upon a grasp of any narrative of which it is a part. I have introduced the concept of narrative in deference to the obvious fact that, in understanding cultural phenomena, people do not deal with the world event by event or with text sentence by sentence. They frame events and sentences in larger structures, whether in the schemata of Bartlett's memory theory, the "plans" of Schank and Abelson, or the "frames" proposed by Van Dijk.[43] These larger structures provide an interpretive context for the components they encompass. So, for example, Elizabeth Bruss and Wolfgang Iser each give a principled description of the "super"-speech-act that constitutes a fictional story, or Philippe Lejeune describes systematically what one undertakes as a writer or reader in entering upon what he has christened "the autobiographical pact."[44] Or one can imagine specifying the conditions on the meanings of particular utterances that follow the initial statement "Let us pray." Under its dispensation, the utterance "Give us this day our daily bread," is not to be taken as a request but, say, as an act of reverence or trust. And, if it is to be understood in its context, it must be interpreted as a trope.

I believe that we shall be able to interpret meanings and meaning-making in a principled manner only in the degree to which we are able to specify the structure and coherence of the larger contexts in which specific meanings are created and transmitted. And that is why I have chosen to end this chapter with a clarification of the issue of meaning. It simply will not do to reject the theoretical centrality of meaning for psychology on the grounds that it is "vague." Its vagueness was in the eye of yesterday's formalistic logician. We are beyond that now.

· CHAPTER THREE ·

Entry into Meaning

IN THE LAST CHAPTER I was particularly concerned to describe what I called "folk psychology"—perhaps "folk human science" would have been a better term. I wanted to show how human beings, in interacting with one another, form a sense of the canonical and ordinary as a background against which to interpret and give narrative meaning to breaches in and deviations from "normal" states of the human condition. Such narrative explications have the effect of framing the idiosyncratic in a "lifelike" fashion that can promote negotiation and avoid confrontational disruption and strife. I presented the case, finally, for a view of cultural meaning-making as a system concerned not solely with sense and reference but with "felicity conditions"—the conditions by which differences in meaning can be resolved by invoking mitigating circumstances that account for divergent interpretations of "reality."

This method of negotiating and renegotiating meanings by the mediation of narrative interpretation is, it seems to me, one of the crowning achievements of human development in the ontogenetic, cultural, and phylogenetic senses of that expression. Culturally, it is enormously aided, of course, by a community's stored narrative resources and its equally precious tool kit of interpretive techniques: its myths, its typology of human plights, but also its traditions for locating and resolving divergent narratives. And phylogenetically, as we shall see in a moment, it is supported in evolution by the emergence in higher primates (even before *Homo*) of a primordial cognitive capacity to recognize and, indeed, to exploit the beliefs and desires of conspecifics—a cognitive capacity that David Premack first called "a theory of mind."[1]

In this chapter, I propose to examine some of the ways in which the young human being achieves (or realizes) the power of narrative, the ability not only to mark what is culturally canonical but to account for deviations that can be incorporated in narrative. The achievement of this skill, as I shall try to show, is not simply a mental achievement, but an achievement of social practice that lends stability to the child's social life. For one of the most powerful forms of social stability, ranking with the well-known system of exchange to which Lévi-Strauss has brought our attention, is the human propensity to share stories of human diversity and to make their interpretations congruent with the divergent moral commitments and institutional obligations that prevail in every culture.[2]

II   But we have a long way to travel before we can deal in such grand generalities. For I propose to discuss how quite young human beings "enter into meaning," how they learn to make sense, particularly narrative sense, of the world around them. The newborn, we say, cannot grasp "meanings." Yet in very short order (and we shall say that this dates from the beginning of language use), he or she is able to do so. So I want to begin this account with a necessary digression into what, for lack of a better term, I must call the "biology of meaning."

The expression at first seems an oxymoron, for meaning itself is a culturally mediated phenomenon that depends upon the prior existence of a shared symbol system. So how can there be a "biology" of meaning? Since C. S. Peirce, we recognize that meaning depends not only upon a sign and a referent but also upon an *interpretant*—a representation of the world in terms of which the sign-referent relationship is mediated.[3] Recall that Peirce distinguished among icon, index, and symbol, the icon bearing a "resemblance" relationship to its referent as with a picture, the index a contingent one as in the relation between smoke and fire, and the symbol depending upon a *system* of signs such that the relation of a sign to its referent is arbitrary and governed only by its position within the system of signs that defines what it "stands for." In this sense, symbols depend upon the existence of a "language" that contains an ordered or rule-governed system of signs.

Symbolic meaning, then, depends in some critical fashion upon the human capacity to internalize such a language and to use its *system* of signs as an interpretant in this "standing for" relationship. The only way in which one might conceive of a biology of meaning, on this view, is by reference to some sort of precursor system that readies the prelinguistic organism to traffic in language, some sort of protolinguistic system. To so conceive the matter would be to invoke innateness, to claim that we have an innate gift for language.

Such appeals to innateness are not new, and they can take many different forms. A generation ago, for example, Noam

Chomsky proposed an innate "language acquisition device" that operated by accepting only those linguistic inputs in the infant's immediate environment that conformed to a postulated deep structure characteristic of all human languages.[4] His notion of deep structure was entirely syntactical and had nothing to do with "meaning" or even with the actual uses of language. It was an entirely linguistic capacity, a *competence* for language. His case rested on the child's alleged ability to grasp the rules of sentence formation and transformation upon exposure to entirely linguistic evidence, even evidence that was not quite sufficient for doing so, evidence that was "degenerate" or "semigrammatical." It made no difference what the sentences meant or how they were used.

In the years since, there has been much ink spilled over Chomsky's claim about innate syntactic readiness. We need not review the history of this controversy, for it concerns us only indirectly. At very least, his claim had the effect of awakening all of us from the sleepy empiricism that had dominated speculation about language acquisition since Augustine. And, besides, it led to a torrent of empirical research on the conditions surrounding the child's acquisition of a mother tongue.[5] From this vast research literature emerged three claims about early acquisition, all of which can guide us in our search for a biology of meaning.

The first is that the child's acquisition of language requires far more assistance from and interaction with caregivers than Chomsky (and many others) had suspected. Language is acquired not in the role of spectator but through use. Being "exposed" to a flow of language is not nearly so important as using it in the midst of "doing." Learning a language, to borrow John Austin's celebrated phrase, is learning "how to do things with words." The child is not learning simply *what* to say but how, where, to whom, and under what circumstances.[6] It is certainly a legitimate occupation for linguists to examine only the parsing rules that characterize *what* a child says from week to week, but in no sense can it provide an account of the conditions upon which language acquisition depends.

The second conclusion is deeply important, and it can be stated simply. Certain communicative functions or intentions are well in place before the child has mastered the formal language for expressing them linguistically. At very least, these include indicating, labeling, requesting, and misleading. Looked at naturalistically, it would seem as if the child were partly motivated to master language in order better to fulfill these functions *in vivo*. Indeed, there are certain generalized communicative skills crucial to language that also seem in place before language proper begins that are later incorporated into the child's speech once it begins: joint attention to a putative referent, turn taking, mutual exchange, to mention the most prominent.

The third conclusion is really a dense summary of the first two: the acquisition of a first language is very context-sensitive, by which is meant that it progresses far better when the child already grasps in some *prelinguistic* way the significance of what is being talked about or of the situation in which the talk is occurring. With an appreciation of context, the child seems better able to grasp not only the lexicon but the appropriate aspects of the grammar of a language.

This leads us right back to our initial query: how does the child "grasp the significance" of situations (or contexts) in a way that can help him or her master the *lexicon and grammar* that fit those situations? What kind of Peircean interpretant can be operating that permits such a grasp? Let me postpone trying to answer this question for a moment in order that I may first make clear what I hope to accomplish.

In the light of the last two decades of research (and particularly with respect to the three generalizations to which this research leads us) I shall propose a very different approach from Chomsky's in dealing with human readiness for language. Without intending to belittle the importance of syntactical form in language, I shall concentrate almost exclusively upon *function* and what I have already called the grasp of context. The subtlety and complexity of syntactic rules lead me to believe that such rules can only be learned *instrumentally*, as instruments for carrying out certain priorly operative functions and objectives. Nowhere in the higher animal kingdom are highly skilled and recombinable acts ever learned "automatically" or by rote, even when they are nurtured by strongly developed biological predispositions—not sexual behavior, not free feeding, not aggression and agonistic behavior, not even spacing.[7] For their full development, they all depend upon being practiced and shaped by use.

Not surprisingly, then, I think the case for how we "enter language" must rest upon a selective set of prelinguistic "readinesses for meaning." That is to say, there are certain classes of meaning to which human beings are innately tuned and for which they actively search. Prior to language, these exist in primitive form as protolinguistic representations of the world whose full realization depends upon the cultural tool of language. Let it be clear that this in no sense denies the claim that there may also be what Derek Bickerton, following Chomsky, calls a "bioprogram" that alerts us to certain syntactical structures.[8] If there is such a bioprogram, its triggering depends not only upon the presence of appropriate exemplars in the linguistic environment of the child but also upon the child's "context sensitivity" that can come only from the kinds of culturally relevant meaning readinesses that I am proposing. It is only *after* some language has been acquired in the formal sense, that one can acquire *further* language as a "bystander." Its initial mastery can come only from participation in language as an instrument of communication.

What then is this prelinguistic readiness for selective classes of meaning? We have characterized it as a form of mental representation. But what is it a representation *of*? I believe it is a highly malleable yet innate representation that is triggered by the acts and expressions of others and by certain basic social contexts in which human beings interact. In a word, we come initially equipped, if not with a "theory" of mind, then surely with a set of predispositions to construe the social world in a particular way and to act upon our construals. This amounts to saying that we come into the world already equipped with a primitive form of folk psychology. We shall return shortly to the nature of the predispositions that constitute it.

I am not the first to suggest that such a form of social "meaning readiness" is a product of our evolutionary past. Indeed, Nicholas Humphrey has proposed that man's readiness for culture may depend upon some such differential "tunedness" to others. And Roger Lewin, reviewing the primate literature of the last decades, concludes that it is probably sensitivity to the requirements of living in groups that provides the criterion for evolutionary selection in high primates.[9] Certainly reviews of shifting and opportunistic primate social coalitions and of the use of "deceit" and "disinformation" in maintaining and augmenting these coalitions speak to prehuman origins of the kinds of folk-psychological representations that I am proposing.[10]

I want to illustrate first what I mean by the claim that a protolinguistic grasp of folk psychology is well in place as a feature of *praxis* before the child is able to express or comprehend the same matters by language. Practical understanding expresses itself first in the child's regulation of social interaction. I draw my illustrative material principally from a well-argued demonstration experiment recently reported by Michael Chandler and his colleagues.

"To hold to a 'theory of mind'," they note, "is to subscribe to a special sort of explanatory framework, common to the folk psychology of most ordinary adults, according to which certain classes of behavior are understood to be predicated upon the particular beliefs and desires subscribed to by those whose actions are in question."[11] There has been a lively debate in the burgeoning literature on "developing theories of mind" as to whether children *have* such theories before the age of four.[12] And as is so often the case in studies of development in children, much of the debate has centered on "how you measure it." If you use a procedure that requires a child to "explain" that somebody *did* something because he or she *believed falsely* that something was the case, and particularly if the child is not involved in the action in question, then children fail in the task until they are four years old. Before that age they seem quite unable to ascribe appropriate actions based on others' false beliefs.[13]

But new evidence provided by Chandler and his colleagues demonstrates that if children are put into a situation where they themselves must prevent somebody else from finding something that they themselves have hidden, then even two-to-three-year-olds will withhold relevant information from the searcher, and even create and then supply the searcher with such *false* information as misleading footprints that lead away from the hidden treasure. The hide-and-seek task, the authors note, "clearly engaged the subject's own self-interests and . . . pitted them against those of another *real* person" and "allowed them to directly *evidence* in action rather than *tell* about . . . false beliefs of others."[14] Nobody doubts that four- or six-year-olds have more mature theories of mind that can encompass what others who are not engaged with them are thinking or desiring. The point, rather, is that even before language takes over as the instrument of interaction one cannot interact *humanly* with others without some protolinguistic "theory of mind." It is inherent in human social behavior and it will express itself in a form appropriate to even a low level of maturity—as when, for example, the nine-month-old looks out along the trajectory of an adult's "point" and, finding nothing there, turns back to check not only the adult's direction of point but the line of visual regard as well. And from this folk psychological antecedent there eventually emerge such linguistic accomplishments as demonstratives, labeling, and the like.[15] Once the child masters through interaction the appropriate prelinguistic forms for managing ostensive reference, he or she can move beyond them to operate, as it were, within the confines of language proper.

III This is not to say that the linguistic forms "grow out of" the prelinguistic practices. It is, I think, impossible in principle to establish any *formal* continuity between an earlier "preverbal" and a later functionally "equivalent" linguistic form. In what sense, for example, is the inverted request syntax of English (as in "Can I have the apple?") "continuous" with the outstretched manual request gesture that predates it? The most we can say in this case is that the two, the gesture and the inverted syntactic structure, fulfill the same function of "requesting." Surely the arbitrary reversal of pronoun and verb is not "requestive" in its own right—neither iconically nor idexically. Syntactic rules bear an *arbitrary* relationship to the functions they fulfill. And there are many different syntactic rules for fulfilling the same function in different languages.

But that is not the whole story. Indeed, it is only half of it. Even granting that grammatical rules are arbitrary with respect to how they fulfill particular functions, may it not be the case that the *order of acquisition* of grammatical forms reflects a priority, as it were, in communicative needs—a priority that reflects a *higher*-level requirement of communicating. The analogy is the mastery of a language's phonology. Phonemes are mastered not for themselves but because they constitute the building blocks of the language's lexemes: they are mastered in the process of mastering lexemic elements. I should like to make the comparable argument that grammatical forms and distinctions are not mastered either for their own sake or merely in the interest of "more efficient communication." Sentences as grammatical entities, while the fetish of the formal grammarian, are not the "natural" units of communication. The natural forms are *discourse units* that fulfill either a "pragmatic" or a "mathetic" discourse function, to use Halliday's terms.[16] Pragmatic functions typically involve getting others to act in our behalf; mathetic ones have to do with, so to speak, "making clear one's thoughts about the world," to use John Dewey's old expression. Both *use* sentences, but neither is limited in any way within the bounds of a sentence. Discourse functions, however, require that certain grammatical forms (however arbitrary) be accessible for their realization, just as "words" in the lexicon depend for their use upon certain arbitrary phonological distinctions being in place.

I have been at great pains to argue (and will argue further later in this chapter) that one of the most ubiquitous and powerful discourse forms in human communication is *narrative*. Narrative structure is even inherent in the praxis of social interaction before it achieves linguistic expression. I want now to make the more radical claim that it is a "push" to construct narrative that determines the order of priority in which grammatical forms are mastered by the young child.[17]

Narrative requires, as mentioned in the preceding chapter, four crucial grammatical constituents if it is to be effectively carried out. It requires, first, a means for emphasizing human action or "agentivity"—action directed toward goals controlled by agents. It requires, secondly, that a sequential order be established and maintained—that events and states be "linearized" in a standard way. Narrative, thirdly, also requires a sensitivity to what is canonical and what violates canonicality in human interaction. Finally, narrative requires something approximating a narrator's perspective: it cannot, in the jargon of narratology, be "voiceless."

If a push to narrative is operative at the discourse level, then the order of the acquisition of grammatical forms should reflect these four requirements. How well does it do so? Fortunately for our quest, much of the work on original language acquisition is described in the meaning-bearing, semantic-relations categories of case grammar. This permits us to assess the kinds of meaning categories to which the young child is initially most sensitive.

Once young children come to grasp the basic idea of reference necessary for any language use—that is, once they can name, can note recurrence, and can register termination of existence—their principal linguistic interest centers on *human action and its outcomes*, particularly *human interaction*. Agent-and-action, action-and-object, agent-and-object, action-and-location, and possessor-and-possession make up the major part of the semantic relations that appear in the first stage of speech.[18] These forms appear not only in referring acts but also in requesting, in effecting exchanges in possession, in giving, and in commenting upon the interaction of others. The young child, moreover, is early and profoundly sensitive to "goals" and their achievement—and to variants of such expressions as "all gone" for completion and "uh oh" for incompletion. People and their actions dominate the child's interest and attention. This is the first requirement of narrative.[19]

A second requirement is early readiness to mark the unusual and to leave the usual unmarked—to concentrate attention and information processing on the offbeat. Young children, indeed, are so easily captivated by the unusual that those of us who conduct research with infants come to count on it. Its power makes possible the "habituation experiment." Infants reliably perk up in the presence of the unusual: they look more fixedly, stop sucking, show cardiac deceleration, and so on.[20] It is not surprising, then, that when they begin acquiring language they are much more likely to devote their linguistic efforts to what is unusual in their world. They not only perk up in the presence of, but also gesture toward, vocalize, and finally talk about what is unusual. As Roman Jakobson told us many years ago, the very act of speaking is an act of marking the unusual from the usual. Patricia Greenfield and Joshua Smith were among the first to demonstrate this important point empirically.[21]

As for the third requirement, "linearizing" and the standardized maintenance of sequence, this is built into the structure of every known grammar.[22] Even at that, it should also be noted that a large part of the known natural grammars of the world render this linearizing task easier by employing the phenomenologically order-preserving SVO (subject-verb-object: "somebody does something") order for indicative sentences. Besides, the SVO forms in a language are the ones first mastered in most cases. Children early start mastering grammatical and lexical forms for "binding" the sequences they recount—by the use of temporals like "then" and "later," and eventually by the use of causals, a matter we shall encounter again presently.

As for the fourth property of narrative, voice or "perspective" (of which we shall also encounter interesting examples later), I suspect it is effected principally by crying and other affective expressions, and also by stress level and similar prosodic features in early speech, rather than by either lexical or grammatical means. But it is surely handled early, as Daniel Stern abundantly demonstrates in his work on "the first relationship."[23]

These four grammatical/lexical/prosodic features, among the earliest to appear, provide the child with an abundant and early armament of narrative tools. My argument, admittedly a radical one, is simply that it is the human push to organize experience narratively that assures the high priority of these features in the program of language acquisition. It is surely worth noting, even if it is almost too self-evident to do so, that children, as a result, produce and comprehend stories, are comforted and alarmed by them, long before they are capable of handling the most fundamental Piagetian logical propositions that can be put into linguistic form. Indeed, we even know from the pathbreaking studies of A. R. Luria and of Margaret Donaldson that logical propositions are most easily comprehended by the child when they are imbedded in an ongoing story. The great Russian folklore morphologist, Vladimir Propp, was among the first to note that the "parts" of a story are, as he put it, *functions* of the story rather than autonomous "themes" or "elements." So one is tempted to ask on the basis of such work as Luria's and Donaldson's whether narratives may not also serve as early interpretants for "logical" propositions before the child has the mental equipment to handle them by such later-developing logical calculi as adult humans can muster.[24]

But while I am arguing that a "protolinguistic" readiness for narrative organization and discourse sets the priority for the order of grammatical acquisition, I am *not* saying that the narrative forms of the culture to which the child early lays claim have no empowering effect on the child's narrative discourse. My argument, rather, and I hope to be able to demonstrate it many times over in the remainder of this chapter, is that while we have an "innate" and primitive predisposition to narrative organization that allows us quickly and easily to comprehend and use it, the culture soon equips us with new powers of narration through its tool kit and through the traditions of telling and interpreting in which we soon come to participate.

IV   In what follows, I want to deal with several different aspects of the socialization of the child's later narrative practices. Let me provide some program notes in advance. I want first, rather as an existence proof, to demonstrate the power of noncanonical events to trigger narrativizing even in quite young children. Then I want very briefly to show how dense and ubiquitous "model" narratives are in the young child's immediate environment. That done, I want next to examine two striking examples of the socialization of narrative in the young child—to show narratively *in vivo* what Chandler and his colleagues demonstrated *in vitro* in their experimental study.[25] Children come to recognize very early on, these examples will show, that what they have done or plan to do will be interpreted not only by the act itself but by how they tell about it. *Logos* and *praxis* are culturally inseparable. The cultural setting of one's *own* actions forces one to be a narrator. The object of the exercise ahead is not only to examine the child's involvement in narrative but to show how greatly this involvement matters to life in the culture.

The demonstration study is a very simple and elegant little experiment with kindergarten children conducted by Joan Lucariello.[26] Its sole aim was to find out what kinds of things tripped off narrative activity in young children between four and five years old. Lucariello told the children a story, either about a standard children's birthday party with presents and candles to be blown out or, in another version, about a visit by a child's same-age cousin and their playing together. Some of the birthday stories violated canonicality—the birthday girl was unhappy, or she poured water on the candles rather than blowing them out, and so on. The violations were designed to introduce imbalances into the Burkean pentad discussed in the previous chapter: between an Agent and an Action or between an Agent and a Scene. There were also comparable variants of the little cousin tale, but since there is no canonical version for such a tale, the variants lacked a real feature of "violation," though they seemed slightly offbeat. After the story, the experimenter asked the children some questions about what had happened in the story they had heard. The first finding was that the anticanonical stories produced a spate of narrative invention by comparison with the canonical one—ten times as many elaborations. One young subject explained the birthday girl's unhappiness by saying she'd probably forgotten the day and didn't have the right dress to wear, another talked about a quarrel with her mother, and so on. Asked point blank why the girl was *happy* in the canonical version, the young subjects were rather nonplussed. All they could think of to say was that it was her birthday, and in some cases they simply shrugged, as if in embarrassment about a grownup's feigned innocence. Even the slightly offbeat versions of the noncanonical "playing cousins" story evoked four times more narrative elaborations than the rather more banal standard one. The elaborations typically took the form discussed in an earlier chapter: they invoked an intentional state (like the birthday girl's confusion about dates) in juxtaposition with a cultural given (the requirement of having a good dress for a party). The narratives were right on target: making sense of a cultural aberration by appeal to a subjective state in a protagonist.

I have not told you about these findings to surprise you. It is their obviousness that interests me. Four-year-olds may not know much about the culture, but they know what's canonical and are eager to provide a tale to account for what is not. Nor is it surprising that they know as much as they do, as a study by Peggy Miller demonstrates.[27]

It concerns the narrative environments of young children in blue-collar Baltimore. Miller recorded conversations at home between mothers and their preschool children, as well as between mothers and other adults within easy earshot of the child. In that intimate environment, the flow of stories recreating everyday experiences is, to paraphrase Miller, "relentless." On average, in every hour of recorded conversation there are 8.5 narratives, one every seven minutes, of which three-quarters are told by the mother. They are simple narratives of a kind widely in everyday use in American talk. It is a form that is usually to be found in child speech by the age of three. It involves a simple orientation, a linear depiction with a precipitating event, a resolution, and sometimes a coda.[28] Since already spoken, they can be understood. A quarter of them are about the child's own doings.

A very considerable number deal with violence, aggression, or threats, and a not inconsiderable number deal explicitly with death, with child abuse, with wife-beatings, and even with shootings. This lack of censorship, this parading of the "harsh realities," is very much part of lower-class Black culture's deliberate emphasis on "toughening" children and readying them early for life. Shirley Brice Heath has reported this same phenomenon in studies of Black children in rural small towns.[29]

The stories, moreover, almost always portray the narrator in a good light. The narrator's triumphs very often take the form of getting the better of somebody in dialogue, and this is exemplified by the use of reported speech, reported speech that is not only dramatic but rhetorically appropriate for a direct and tough presentation of self, as in this fragment: "And she says, 'Look at that big nosed B-I-T-C-H.' And I turned and I says, 'Uh, you talkin to me?' I said, 'ARE YOU TALKIN TO ME?' I says, 'Well, you fat slob, I put you in a skillet and strip you down to normal size, if you mess with me.' "[30] The corpus contains few examples of "telling stories on oneself." The emphasis is on the perils to Agentivity in a tough world and how one copes in that world by deed and by word. And in the few instances where Miller was fortunate enough to record young children retelling stories that had been earlier recorded in the adult version, the children exaggerated both the drama and the dramatizing paralinguistic features of the originals.

I do not mean to single out blue-collar children in Baltimore as having a special narrative environment. All narrative environments are specialized for cultural needs, all stylize the narrator as a form of Self, all define kinds of relations between narrator and interlocutor. I could have used Shirley Brice Heath's account of literal, bowdlerized narrating in White small-town Roadville.[31] Any closely examined sample of such narrative environments will tell much the same story of the ubiquitousness of narratives in the world of children (and the world of adults, for that matter) and of its functional importance in bringing children into the culture.

V   Now we can turn to the uses to which children put their narratives, and there is no better place to begin than with Judy Dunn's book *The Beginnings of Social Understanding*. "Children," Dunn says, "have rarely been studied in the world in which these developments take place, or in a context in which we can be sensitive to the subtleties of their social understanding."[32] But hers is not simply a naturalist's plea for "ecological situatedness" in psychological research. Her point, rather, is that social understanding, however abstract it may eventually become, always begins as *praxis* in particular contexts in which the child is a *protagonist*—an agent, a victim, an accomplice. The child learns to play a part in everyday family "drama" *before* there is ever any telling or justifying or excusing required. What is permissible and what not, what leads to what outcomes—these are first learned in action. The transformation of such enactive knowledge into language comes only later, and as we already know from previous discussion, the child is linguistically sensitive to just such action-tagged "referential targets." But there is something else that characterizes the speech acts of young children talking about the interactions in which they are involved, something that Dunn brings to our attention, that is especially important.

Young children often hear accounts of their own interactions from older siblings or parents, accounts that are constituted in terms of the familiar Burkean pentad: an Agent's Action toward a Goal by some Instrumentality in a particular constraining Scene.[33] But the account is given in a form that runs counter to their own interpretation and interest. It is often from the point of view of another protagonist's goal that may be either in conflict with their own version of "what happened" or at variance with their version of "the Trouble." Narrative accounts, under these circumstances, are no longer neutral. They have rhetorical aims or illocutionary intentions that are not merely expository but rather partisan, designed to put the case if not adversarially then at least convincingly in behalf of a particular interpretation. In those early family

85

conflicts, narrative becomes an instrument for telling not only what happened but also why it justified the action recounted. As with narrative generally, "what happened" is tailored to meet the conditions on "so what."

Dunn sees this as a reflection, so to speak, of "family politics," a politics not of high Freudian drama but of daily necessity. The child, in the nature of things, has her own desires, but given her reliance upon the family for affection, these desires often create conflict when they collide with the wishes of parents and siblings. The child's task when conflict arises is to balance her own desires against her commitment to others in the family. And she learns very soon that action is not enough to achieve this end. Telling the right story, putting her actions and goals in a legitimizing light, is just as important. Getting what you want very often means getting the right story. As John Austin told us many years ago in his famous essay "A Plea for Excuses," a justification rests on a story of mitigating circumstances.[34] But to get the story right, to pit yours successfully against your younger brother's, requires knowing what constitutes the canonically acceptable version. A "right" story is one that connects your version through mitigation with the canonical version.

So, like the young children in Baltimore, these children too come to understand "everyday" narrative not only as a form of recounting but also as a form of rhetoric. By their third and fourth years, we see them learning how to use their narratives to cajole, to deceive, to flatter, to justify, to get what they can without provoking a confrontation with those they love. And they are en route as well to becoming connoisseurs of story genres that do the same. To put the matter in terms of speech-act theory, knowing the generative structure of nar-

rative enables them to construct locutions to fit the requirements of a wide range of illocutionary intentions. This same
set of skills also equips these young children with a more
discerning empathy. They often are able to interpret for their
parents the meanings and intentions of younger siblings who
are trying to make a case for themselves—especially when
there is no conflict of interest involved.

To recapitulate, then, a grasp of quotidian "family drama"
comes first in the form of *praxis*. The child, as we already
know, soon masters the linguistic forms for referring to actions and their consequences as they occur. She learns soon
after that what you do is drastically affected by how you recount what you are doing, will do, or have done. Narrating
becomes not only an expository act but a rhetorical one. To
narrate in a way that puts your case convincingly requires not
only language but a mastery of the canonical forms, for one
must make one's actions seem an extension of the canonical,
transformed by mitigating circumstances. In the process of
achieving these skills, the child learns to use some of the less
attractive tools of the rhetorical trade—deceit, flattery, and
the rest. But she also learns many of the useful forms of interpretation and thereby develops a more penetrating empathy.
And so she enters upon human culture.

VI   Now move backward in developmental time—to
Emily, whose soliloquies, recorded between her eighteenth
month and third year, became the subject of a book, *Narratives
from the Crib*.[35] For all her tender years, she was in the midst
of life. A brother, Stephen, was born and displaced her not
only from her solo role in the family but from her very room

and crib. If, as Vladimir Propp once remarked, folktales begin in lack and displacement, this was surely a "narratogenic" time for Emily.[36] And shortly after the arrival of her brother, she was introduced to the boisterous life of nursery school. With both parents working, there were babysitters as well—all against the background of an ill-planned city where even the carpool pickups could become tense and erratic. "In the midst of life" is not an exaggeration.

It was our good fortune that Emily was steadily improving in her use of her native language while all these momentous events in her life were taking place. For it allowed us to observe the growth of her language not only as a communicative instrument but also as a vehicle for reflecting aloud when her busy days were over. Her soliloquies were rich. Indeed, contrary to an "established" Vygotskyan principle, they were grammatically more complex, more extended in utterance length, and less "here-and-now" than her conversational speech—probably because when talking to herself she did not have to fit her speech into the interstices of an interrupting interlocutor's remarks.

Why do any of us talk to ourselves? And why especially a young child, albeit a somewhat precocious young child? John Dewey proposed that language provides a way of sorting out our thoughts about the world, and there are chapters in *Narratives from the Crib* confirming his conjecture. We shall come back to such matters presently. Emily also talks to her stuffed animals and gives variorum recitals of favorite books that have been read to her or of songs she has learned. About a quarter of her soliloquies were straightforward narrative accounts: autobiographical narratives about what she had been doing or what she thought she would be up to tomorrow. Listening to the tapes and reading the transcripts repeatedly, we were struck by the *constitutive* function of her monologic narrative. She was not simply reporting; she was trying to make sense of her everyday life. She seemed to be in search of an integral structure that could encompass what she had *done* with what she *felt* with what she *believed*.

Because the lexico-grammatical speech of almost all children improves steadily during the early years of life, we too easily take it for granted that language acquisition is "autonomous." According to this dogma, part of the Chomskian heritage discussed earlier, language acquisition needs no motive other than itself, no particularly specialized support from the environment, nothing except the unfolding of some sort of self-charged "bioprogram." But looking closely at the transcripts and listening to the tapes, there were times when we had the irresistible impression that Emily's leaps forward in speech were fueled by a need to construct meaning, more particularly narrative meaning. Granted that the achievement of meaning requires the use of a grammar and a lexicon, the search for it may not. Lois Bloom, like us, remarked at the conclusion of one of her own studies that, for example, the child's mastery of causal expressions seemed to be driven by an interest in the reasons *why* people did things. In the same sense, Emily's push to better grammatical construction and a more extended lexicon seemed to be impelled by a need to get things organized in an appropriate serial order, to get them marked for their specialness, to take some sort of stance on them. No doubt, in time children become interested in language for its own sake, almost as a form of play. Like Ruth Weir's Anthony, Emily seemed to be "only playing with language" in some of her later monologues, but even then there seemed to be something else as well.[37] So what might it be?

We say in developmental linguistics that "function precedes form." There are, for example, gestural forms of requesting and indicating well *before* there is lexico-grammatical speech for expressing these functions, and prelinguistic intentions to request or indicate seem to guide the search for and hasten the mastery of the appropriate linguistic forms. And so it must be with the child's push to give meaning or "structure" to experience. Much of Emily's early acquisition seemed to be driven by a need to fix and to express narrative structure—the order of human events and what difference they made to the narrator/protagonist. I know this is not the standard version of language acquisition, but let me spell out the details.

The three most notable and earliest accomplishments in Emily's narrative soliloquies were all in the interest of fixing her narratives more firmly into language. First, there was a steady mastery of linguistic forms to achieve more linear and tighter sequencing in her accounts of "what happened." Her early accounts began by stringing together happenings by the use of simple conjunctions, moved then to reliance upon temporals like *and then,* and passed finally to the use of causals like her ubiquitous *because.* Why is she so finicky about ordering, even to the extent of correcting herself at times about who or what preceded or followed whom or what? After all, she is only talking to herself. William Labov comments in his landmark paper on narrative structure that the meaning of "what happened" is strictly determined by the order and form of its sequence.[38] It is this meaning that Emily seems to be after.

Second, her interest in and achievement of forms for distinguishing the canonical or ordinary from the unusual showed rapid progress. Words like *sometimes* and *always* came into her soliloquies by her second year, and were used with deliberation and stress. She showed a consuming interest in what she took to be steady, reliable, and ordinary, and knowledge of this ordinariness served as a background for explicating the exceptional. She worked deliberately to get such matters clear. In this respect, she is much like the children in Dunn's Cambridge study.

Moreover, once Emily had established and expressed what was quantitatively reliable, she began introducing a note of deontic necessity. *Got to* entered her lexicon and served to mark those events that were not only frequent but, as it were, *comme il faut,* as when she announced in one soliloquy after an air trip to her grandmother's that you "got to have luggage" to get on an airplane. And it was at this point in her development that she began using the timeless present tense for marking ritual canonical events. It no longer sufficed to recount a Sunday breakfast as *Daddy did make some cornbread for Emmy have.* Sundays were now a species of timeless event: *when you wake up, but on Sunday mornings sometimes we wake up . . . sometime we wake up morning.* Such timeless accounts double in relative frequency between 22 and 33 months. They have a special significance to which we shall turn presently.

Third and finally, there was Emily's introduction of personal perspective and evaluation into her narrative accounts, the standard way of adding a landscape of consciousness to the landscape of action in narrative. She did this increasingly over the period during which we monitored her soliloquies, most usually in the form of expressing her feelings about what she was recounting. But she also set out an epistemic perspective, as for example about her not being able to figure out why her father was not accepted in the local marathon. She seemed to distinguish quite clearly in her late soliloquies between her own doubts (*I think maybe . . .*) and states of uncertainty in the world (*sometimes Carl come play*). The two have distinctive meanings in her soliloquies: one is about the state of mind of the Actor-Narrator (that is, the autobiographer); the other is about the Scene. They are both perspectival. Both deal with the "so what" of the recounted happenings.

The engine of all this linguistic effort is not so much a push toward logical coherence, though that is not absent. It is, rather, a need to "get the story right": who did what to whom where, was it the "real" and steady thing or a rogue happening, and how do I feel about it. Her language aided but did not *compel* her to talk and think in this way. She was using a *genre*, one that came to her easily and, perhaps, naturally. But she already had another genre in hand that she was using and perfecting, as we learn from Carol Feldman's analysis of Emily's problem-solving soliloquies.[39] In these, Emily occupies herself with the shifting world of categories and causation, of attributes and identities, with the domain of "reasons why." This genre, as Feldman describes it, "has a tidy and intricate pattern of puzzles posed, considerations raised, and solutions achieved." Take the following example of Emily's trying to figure out why her father had been turned down for that marathon:

> Today Daddy went, trying to get into the race, but the people said no so he has to watch it on television. I don't know why that is, maybe cause there's too many people. I think that's why, why he couldn't go in it . . . I wish I can watch him. I

wish I could watch him. But they said no, no, no, Daddy, Daddy, Daddy. No, no, no. Have to, have to watch on television.

Eventually, of course, Emily (like the rest of us) learns to interdigitate these two basic genres, using each to clarify or adumbrate on the other. Here, again at 32 months, is a striking example. Note that the narrative portion is still principally concerned with canonicality rather than exceptionality, but note that the canonicality is being imposed upon a still somewhat troubling event: being left by a parent, albeit at nursery school:

> Tomorrow when we wake up from bed, first me and Daddy and Mommy, you, eat breakfast eat breakfast, like we *usually* do, and then we're going to p-l-a-y, and then soon as Daddy comes, Carl's going to come over and then we're going to play a little while. And then Carl and Emily are both going down the car with somebody, and /we're going to ride to nursery school/ [whispered], and then when we *get* there, we're *all* going to get out of the car, and go *into* nursery school, and Daddy's going to give us kisses, then go, and then say, and then he will say good*bye*, then he's going to go to work, and we're going to play at *nur*sery school. Won't that be funny?

And then immediately she shifts into her puzzle-solving genre:

> Because sometimes I go to *nur*sery school cause it's a nursery school day. Sometimes I stay with Tanta all week. And sometimes we play Mom and Dad. But usually, sometimes, I um, oh go to nursery school.

So Emily by her third year masters the forms for putting sequence, canonicality, and perspective at the service of her push to narrativize her experience. The genre serves to organize her experience of human interactions in a lifelike, story-like way. Her narrative environment is, in its own way, as distinctive as the environments of the Black ghetto children in Baltimore. In her case, we learn from her pre-soliloquy exchanges with her parents, there is enormous stress on "getting things right," on being able to give "reasons," and on understanding the options open to her. Her parents, after all, are academics. Like the children in Dunn's Cambridge, moreover, Emily also learns to talk and to think rhetorically, to design her utterances more convincingly to express her stance.

In time, as we saw, she imports another genre into her narratives—problem-solving. And in short order, this generic importation becomes like an *obbligato* in her narratives. I use the musical terms advisedly: an *obbligato,* as the Oxford Dictionary puts it, is something "that cannot be omitted . . . a part essential to the completeness of the composition." It is not that narrative and paradigmatic modes of discourse fuse, for they do not. It is, rather, that the logical or paradigmatic mode is brought to bear on the task of explicating the breach in the narrative. The explication is in the form of "reasons," and it is interesting that these reasons are often stated in the timeless present tense, better to distinguish them from the course of events in the past. But when reasons are used in this way, they must be made to seem not only logical but lifelike as well, for the requirements of narrative still dominate. This is the critical intersection where verifiability and verisimilitude seem to come together. To bring off a successful convergence is to bring off good rhetoric. The next big advances in our understanding of language acquisition will probably be achieved when that dark subject is enlightened by developmental research.

VII   The view I have been proposing is an interpretivist one, interpretivist in its view of the activities of those who practice the human sciences and of those whom they study. It takes the position that what makes a cultural community is *not* just shared beliefs about what people are like and what the world is like or how things should be valued. There must obviously be some consensus to ensure the achievement of civility. But what may be just as important to the coherence of a culture is the existence of interpretive procedures for adjudicating the different construals of reality that are inevitable in any diverse society. Michelle Rosaldo is surely right about the solidarity created by a cultural stock of story plights and story characters.[40] But I doubt it suffices. Let me explain.

It is probably the case that human beings forever suffer conflicts of interest, with attendant grudges, factions, coalitions, and shifting alliances. But what is interesting about these fractious phenomena is not how much they separate us but how much more often they are neutralized or forgiven or excused. The primatologist Frans de Waal warns that ethologists have tended to exaggerate the aggressiveness of primates (including man) while undervaluing (and underobserving) the myriad means by which these higher species keep peace.[41] In human beings, with their astonishing narrative gift, one of the principal forms of peacekeeping is the human gift for presenting, dramatizing, and explicating the mitigating circumstances surrounding conflict-threatening breaches in the ordinariness of life. The objective of such narrative is not to reconcile, not to legitimize, not even to excuse, but rather to explicate. And the explications offered in the ordinary telling of such narratives are not always forgiving of the protagonist depicted.

Rather, it is the narrator who usually comes off best. But however that may be, narrativizing makes the happening comprehensible against the background of ordinariness we take as the basic state of life—even if what has been made comprehensible is no more lovable as a result. To be in a viable culture is to be bound in a set of connecting stories, connecting even though the stories may not represent a consensus.

When there is a breakdown in a culture (or even within a microculture like the family) it can usually be traced to one of several things. The first is a deep disagreement about what constitutes the ordinary and canonical in life and what the exceptional or divergent. And this we know in our time from what one might call the "battle of life-styles," exacerbated by intergenerational conflict. A second threat inheres in the rhetorical overspecialization of narrative, when stories become so ideologically or self-servingly motivated that distrust displaces interpretation, and "what happened" is discounted as fabrication. On the large scale, this is what happens under a totalitarian regime, and contemporary novelists of Central Europe have documented it with painful exquisiteness—Milan Kundera, Danilo Kis, and many others.[42] The same phenomenon expresses itself in modern bureaucracy, where all except the official story of what is happening is silenced or stonewalled. And finally, there is breakdown that results from sheer impoverishment of narrative resources—in the permanent underclass of the urban ghetto, in the second and third generation of the Palestinian refugee compound, in the hunger-preoccupied villages of semipermanently drought-stricken villages in sub-Saharan Africa. It is not that there is a total loss in putting story form to experience, but that the "worst scenario" story comes so to dominate daily life that variation seems no longer to be possible.

I hope this does not seem too far afield from the detailed analysis of early narrativizing with which the bulk of this chapter has been concerned. I have wanted to make it clear that our capacity to render experience in terms of narrative is not just child's play, but an instrument for making meaning that dominates much of life in culture—from soliloquies at bedtime to the weighing of testimony in our legal system. In the end, indeed, it is not so startling that Ronald Dworkin should liken the process of legal interpretation to literary interpretation and that many students of jurisprudence have joined him in this view.[43] Our sense of the normative is nourished in narrative, but so is our sense of breach and of exception. Stories make "reality" a mitigated reality. Children, I think, are predisposed naturally and by circumstance to start their narrative careers in that spirit. And we equip them with models and procedural tool kits for perfecting those skills. Without those skills we could never endure the conflicts and contradictions that social life generates. We would become unfit for the life of culture.

CHAPTER FOUR

Autobiography and Self

W HAT I SHOULD LIKE to do in this final chapter is to illustrate what I have been calling "cultural psychology." I want to do this by applying its way of thought to a classically central concept in psychology. The concept I have chosen for this exercise is "the Self"—as central, classical, and intractable as any in our conceptual lexicon. Does a cultural psychology shed any light on this difficult topic?

As a *qualia* of "direct" human experience, Self has a peculiarly tortured history. Some of the theoretical trouble it has generated, I suspect, can be attributed to the "essentialism" that has often marked the quest for its elucidation, as if Self were a substance or an essence that preexisted our effort to describe it, as if all one had to do was to inspect it in order to discover its nature. But the very notion of doing this is itself suspect on many grounds. What finally led E. B. Titchener's favorite intellectual son, Edwin G. Boring, to give up the whole introspective enterprise was precisely this—that, as he taught us as graduate students, introspection is at best "early retrospection," and subject to the same kinds of selectivity and construction as any other kind of memory.[1] Introspection is as subject to "top down" schematization as memory.

So what emerged as an alternative to the idea of a directly observable Self was the notion of a conceptual Self, self as a concept created by reflection, a concept constructed much as we construct other concepts. But "self-realism" lingered on.[2] For the question now became whether the *concept* of Self thus constructed was a *true* concept, whether it reflected the "real" or essential self. Psychoanalysis, of course, was a principal essentialist sinner: its topography of ego, superego, and id was the *real* thing, and the method of psychoanalysis was the electron microscope that laid it bare.

Ontological questions about the "conceptual Self" were soon replaced by a more interesting set of concerns: By what processes and in reference to what kinds of experience do human beings formulate their own concept of Self, and what kinds of Self do they formulate? Does "Self" comprise (as William James had implied) an "extended" self incorporating one's family, friends, possessions, and so on?[3] Or, as Hazel Markus and Paula Nurius suggested, are we a colony of Possible Selves, including some that are feared and some hoped for, all crowding to take possession of a Now Self?[4]

I suspect that there was also something even more pervasive in the intellectual climate that led to the demise of realism in our view of the Self. It occurred during a half-century that had also witnessed the comparable rise of antirealism in modern physics, of skeptical perspectivalism in modern philosophy, of constructivism in the social sciences, the proposal of "paradigm shifts" in intellectual history. With metaphysics increasingly out of fashion, epistemology became, as it were, its secular counterpart: so long as ontological ideas could be converted into issues in the nature of knowing, they were palatable. In consequence, the Essential Self gave way to the Conceptual Self with hardly a shot fired.[5]

Freed of the shackles of ontological realism, a new set of concerns about the nature of Self began to emerge, rather more "transactional" concerns. Is not Self a transactional relationship between a speaker and an Other, indeed, a Generalized Other?[6] Is it not a way of framing one's consciousness, one's position, one's identity, one's commitment with respect to another? Self, in this dispensation, becomes "dialogue dependent," designed as much for the recipient of our discourse as for intrapsychic purposes.[7] But these efforts at a cultural psychology had a very limited effect on psychology in general.

I think that what kept psychology from continuing to develop steadily along these promising lines was its stubborn antiphilosophical stance that kept it isolated from currents of thought in its neighboring disciplines in the human sciences. Rather than finding common cause with our neighbors in defining such central ideas as "mind" or "Self," we in psychology preferred to rely upon standardized research paradigms to "define" our "own" concepts. We take these research paradigms to be the operations that define the concept we are studying—tests, experimental procedures, and the like. In time, these methods become proprietary, as it were, and come rigidly to define the phenomenon in question: "Intelligence *is* what intelligence tests measure." And so with the study of Self: "it" is whatever is measured by tests of the self-concept. So there has grown up a thriving testing industry built around a set of narrowly defined self-concepts each with its own test, and with a recent two-volume handbook given over more to methodological complexities than to substantive issues.[8] Each test creates its own disconnected module of research, each to be taken as an "aspect" of some larger notion of Self that is left unspecified.

Even the best of this work has suffered from being yoked to its own testing paradigm. Take, for example, the aspect of Self embodied in studies of "level of aspiration"—measured by asking subjects to predict how well they would do on a task after having succeeded or failed on a similar task on previous trials. Initially formulated by Kurt Lewin, the idea was at least theoretically located in his system of thought. It generated much research, some of it quite interesting. I suspect it died of its singular laboratory paradigm. It had become too procedurally "hardened" to be broadened, say, into a general theory of "self-esteem," and it was surely too insulated to be incorporated into a more general theory of Self.[9] Besides, it grew without much of a mind for the broader conceptual developments that were taking place in the other human sciences—antipositivism, transactionalism, and emphasis upon context.

This has changed now—or at least, it is in process of changing. But it will help us to appreciate this change, I think, to track a comparable change in another germinal concept of psychology, one that on the surface might seem quite separate from the concept of self. It might serve to show how developments within the broader intellectual community can eventually work their way even into those narrow channels in which our standard experimental paradigms navigate. Let me take as my exemplary case the recent history of the concept of "learning" and try to show how eventually it became absorbed into the broader culture of ideas, as it came to be redefined as the study of "the acquisition of knowledge." It contains fascinating little parallels (or are they counterparts?) to our topic of Self.

One has to begin with "animal learning" because that was the paradigmatic amphitheater in which, for at least a half-century, the major embattled issues of learning theory were fought out. Within that sphere, contending theories built their models of the learning process on particular paradigm procedures for studying learning, even to the extent of devising ones that met the specialized requirement of working with a particular species. Clark Hull and his students, for example, chose the multiple T-maze as their favored instrument. It was well-suited to the rat and to the measurement of the cumulative effects of terminal reinforcement in reducing errors. Hullian theory, in effect, was designed to accommodate the findings generated by this research paradigm. In spite of its draconian behaviorism, "Yale learning theory" had even to generate a mechanistic simulacrum of teleology to explain why errors nearer to the end of the maze (where the reward was) were eliminated sooner in learning. One lived with one's paradigm! Edward Tolman, more cognitive and "purposivist" in his approach, also used rats and mazes (almost as if to carry the game into Hull's court), but he and his students favored open-strip mazes in a rich visual environment rather than the closed-in alley mazes favored by Hull at Yale. The Californians wanted their animals to have access to a wider range of cues, especially spatial ones outside the maze. Tolman's theory, not surprisingly, ended up likening learning to the construction of a map, a "cognitive map" that represented the world of possible "means-end relations." Hull's ended with a theory that treated the cumulative effects of reinforcement in "strengthening" responses to stimuli. In the language of those

103

times, Tolman's was a "map room" theory, Hull's a "switch-board" theory.[10]

Now obviously, research on *anything* will yield findings that mirror its procedures for observing or measuring. Science always invents a conforming reality in just that way. When we "confirm" our theory by "observations," we devise procedures that will favor the theory's plausibility. Anyone who objects can poach on our theory by devising variants of our very own procedures to demonstrate exceptions and "disproofs." And that was how the battles of learning theory were fought. So, for example, I. Krechevsky could show that Yale behavior theory had to be wrong by demonstrating that rats in T-mazes were impelled by seemingly self-generated "hypotheses" of many kinds, including right-turning or left-turning ones, and that reinforcements *only* worked for responses driven by hypotheses that were in force at the time—which meant that reinforcement was really only "confirmation of a hypothesis." But radical shifts rarely result from such infighting, though the difference between a theory of response reinforcement and a theory of hypothesis confirmation was by no means trivial. In retrospect, indeed, the battle over "hypothesis versus chance reinforcement" might even seem like a precursor to the cognitive revolution. But so long as the *locus classicus* of the dispute was the rat maze, open strip or closed alley, it remained a precursor without consequences.

In the end, "learning theory" died, or perhaps it would be better to say it withered away, leaving behind principally traces of technology. Boredom played its usual healthy role: the debates became too specialized to be of much general interest. But two historical movements were already in progress that, in a decade or two, would marginalize "classical" learning theory. One was the cognitive revolution, the other transactionalism. The cognitive revolution simply absorbed the concept of learning into the broader concept of "the acquisition of knowledge." Even the efforts of learning theory to broaden its base by attempting to reduce theories of personality to its terms were brought to a halt—a matter that will concern us again later. Before that revolution, theories of personality had concentrated almost exclusively upon motivation, affect, and their transformations—matters that seemed to be within reach of learning theory. Indeed, there was a period in the 1940s when such "learning theory translations became almost a cottage industry."[11] But with the advent of the cognitive revolution, emphasis in personality theory also shifted to more cognitive matters—for example, what kinds of "personal constructs" people used for making sense of their worlds and of themselves.[12]

But the second historical movement to which I alluded above had not yet reached psychology—the new transactional contextualism that was expressing itself in sociology and anthropology in such doctrines as "ethnomethodology" and the other developments discussed in Chapter 2. It was the view that human action could not be fully or properly accounted for from the inside out—by reference only to intrapsychic dispositions, traits, learning capacities, motives, or whatever. Action required for its explication that it be *situated,* that it be conceived of as continuous with a cultural world. The realities that people constructed were *social* realities, negotiated with others, distributed between them. The social world in which we lived was, so to speak, neither "in the head" nor "out there" in some positivistic aboriginal form. And both mind and the Self were part of that social world. If the cognitive revolution erupted in 1956, the contextual revolution (at least in psychology) is occurring today.

Consider first how contextualism affects ideas about knowledge and how we acquire it. As Roy Pea, David Perkins, and others now put it, a "person's" knowledge is not *just* in one's own head, in "person solo," but in the notes that one has put into accessible notebooks, in the books with underlined passages on one's shelves, in the handbooks one has learned how to consult, in the information sources one has hitched up to the computer, in the friends one can call up to get a reference or a "steer," and so on almost endlessly. All of these, as Perkins points out, are parts of the knowledge flow of which one has become a part. And that flow even includes those highly conventionalized forms of rhetoric that we use for justifying and explaining what we are doing, each tailored to and "scaffolded" by the occasion of use. Coming to know anything, in this sense, is both *situated* and (to use the Pea-Perkins term) *distributed*.[13] To overlook this situated-distributed nature of knowledge and knowing is to lose sight not only of the cultural nature of knowledge but of the correspondingly cultural nature of knowledge acquisition.

Ann Brown and Joseph Campione add another dimension to this picture of distribution. Schools, they note, are themselves "communities of learning or thinking" in which there are procedures, models, feedback channels, and the like that determine how, what, how much, and in what form a child "learns." The word *learns* deserves its quotation marks, since what the learning child is doing is participating in a kind of cultural geography that sustains and shapes what he or she is doing, and without which there would, as it were, be *no* learning. As David Perkins puts it at the end of his discussion, perhaps the "proper person is better conceived . . . not as the pure and enduring nucleus but [as] the sum and swarm of participations."[14] At one stroke, the "learning theories" of the 1930s are put into a new distributive perspective.[15]

The incoming tide was soon lapping around psychology's quest for Self.[16] Is Self to be taken as an enduring, subjective nucleus, or might it too be better conceived as "distributed"? In fact, the "distributive" conception of Self was not that new *outside* psychology: it had a long tradition in historical and anthropological scholarship, that is, in the ancient tradition of interpretive history and in the newer but growing tradition of interpretivism in cultural anthropology. I have in mind, of course, works like Karl Joachim Weintraub's historical study of individuality, *The Value of the Individual*, and E. R. Dodd's classic *The Greeks and the Irrational*, and more recently, Michelle Rosaldo's anthropological study of "Self" among the Ilongot and Fred Myers's of the Pintupi "Self." And one should mention work addressing more particular historical questions such as Brian Stock's query about whether the introduction of "silent reading" might not have changed Western conceptions of Self or the work of the French *Annales* school on the history of private life. Later we shall be concerned with the monumental studies of the latter addressing the deep question of whether the "history of privacy" in the Western world might not also be considered an exercise in understanding the emergence of the Western Self.[17] What all these works have in common is the aim (and virtue) of *locating* Self not in the fastness of immediate private consciousness but in a cultural-historical situation as well. Nor, as already noted, are contemporary social philosophers far behind in this regard. For no sooner had they begun to question the previously

accepted hold of positivist verificationism on the social sciences—the notion that there is an "objective" and free-
standing reality whose truth can be discovered by appropriate
methods—than it became clear that Self too must be treated
as a construction that, so to speak, proceeds from the outside
in as well as from the inside out, from culture to mind as well
as from mind to culture.

If not "verifiable" in the positivist psychologist's hard-nosed
sense, at least these frankly interpretive anthropological and
historical studies could be scrutinized for their plausibility.
And even so austere a guardian of the methodological purity
of psychology as Lee Cronbach reminds us that "Validity is
subjective rather than objective: the plausibility of the conclusion is what counts. And plausibility, to twist a cliché, lies in
the ear of the beholder."[18] Validity, in short, is an interpretive
concept, not an exercise in research design.

Let me sketch briefly how this new thrust seems to have
found its way into mainstream contemporary conceptions of
the Self. I shall not be able to do full justice to it here, but I
can say enough to indicate why (at least in my view) it marks
a new turn in what is meant by a cultural psychology, one I
hope to be able to illustrate further in the second half of this
chapter.

The new view initially erupted as a protest against a spe-
cious objectivism both in social psychology and in the study
of personality. Kenneth Gergen was one of the earliest among
the social psychologists to sense how social psychology might
be changed by the adoption of an interpretivist, constructivist,
and "distributive" view of psychological phenomena, and
some of his earliest work was directed specifically toward the
construction of Self. In this work of two decades ago, he set

out to show how people's self-esteem and their self-concept changed in sheer reaction to the kinds of people they found themselves among, and changed even more in response to the positive or negative remarks that people made to them. Even if they were asked merely to play a particular public role in a group, their self-image often changed in a fashion to be congruent with that role. Indeed, in the presence of others who were older or seen to be more powerful than they were, people would report on "Self" in a quite different and diminished way from their manner of seeing themselves when in the presence of younger or less-esteemed people. And interacting with egotists led them to see themselves one way, with the self-effacing, another.[19] In the distributive sense, then, the Self can be seen as a product of the situations in which it operates, the "swarms of its participations," as Perkins puts it.

Gergen insisted, moreover, that these "results" could in no way be generalized beyond the historical occasions in which they were obtained. "None of these findings should be viewed as trans-historically reliable. Each depended to a major extent upon the investigator's knowledge of what conceptual shifts were subject to alteration within a given historical context."[20] But, he added, there *are* two generalities that need, nonetheless, to be taken into account in interpreting findings such as these: both of them universals having to do with man's way of orienting toward culture and the past. The first is human *reflexivity*, our capacity to turn around on the past and alter the present in its light, or to alter the past in the light of the present. Neither the past nor the present stays fixed in the face of this reflexivity. The "immense repository" of our past encounters may be rendered salient in different ways as we review them reflexively, or may be changed by reconceptual-

109

ization.[21] The second universal is our "dazzling" intellectual capacity to *envision alternatives*—to conceive of other ways of being, of acting, of striving. So while it may be the case that in some sense we are "creatures of history," in another sense we are autonomous agents as well. The Self, then, like any other aspect of human nature, stands both as a guardian of permanence and as a barometer responding to the local cultural weather. The culture, as well, provides us with guides and stratagems for finding a niche between stability and change: it exhorts, forbids, lures, denies, rewards the commitments that the Self undertakes. And the Self, using its capacities for reflection and for envisaging alternatives, escapes or embraces or reevaluates and reformulates what the culture has on offer. Any effort to understand the nature and origins of Self is, then, an interpretive effort akin to that used by a historian or an anthropologist trying to understand a "period" or a "people." And ironically enough, once an official history or anthropology has been proclaimed in a culture and enters the public domain, that very fact alters the process of Self-construction. Not surprisingly, the first of Gergen's essays to catch the attention of his fellow social psychologists was entitled "Social Psychology as History."[22]

Gergen—like Garfinkel, Schutz, and the others whose "ethno-" programs in sociology and anthropology we encountered in Chapter 2—was initially interested in the "rules" by which we construct and negotiate social realities. The ego or Self was envisaged as some mix of decisionmaker, strategist, and gamesman figuring its commitments, even including the commitment, to use Erving Goffman's phrase, of how to present Self to Others. This was an exceedingly calculating and intellectual view of Self, and I think that it reflected some of the rationalism of the early cognitive revolution.[23] It was probably the rising revolt against verificationist epistemology that freed social scientists to explore other ways of conceiving of Self aside from looking at it as a reckoning agent governed by logical rules. But that brings us to the next part of the story.

By the late 1970s and early 1980s, the notion of Self as a storyteller came on the scene—the Self telling stories that included a delineation of Self as part of the story. I suspect that literary theory and new theories of narrative cognition provoked the shift. But this is not the place to examine that interesting transition in the human sciences.[24] In any case, it was not long before narrative was at the center of the stage.

Donald Spence was surely (along with Roy Schafer, to whom we shall come presently) among the first on the scene.[25] Speaking from within psychoanalysis, Spence addressed the question of whether a patient in analysis *recovered* the past from memory in the sense in which an archaeologist digs up artifacts of a buried civilization, or whether, rather, analysis enabled one to *create* a new narrative that, though it might be only a screen memory or even a fiction, was still close enough to the real thing to start a reconstructive process going. The "truth" that mattered, so went his argument, was not the historical truth but something he chose to call the *narrative* truth. Such narrative truth, screen memory or fiction though it might be, succeeds if it fits the patient's "real" story, if it somehow manages to capture within *its* code the patient's *real* trouble.[26]

For Spence, then, the ego (or Self) is cast in the role of a storyteller, a constructor of narratives about a life. The analyst's task is to help the patient in the construction of this narrative, a narrative with a Self at its center. There is an unresolved difficulty in this account. For, according to Spence, neither the analyst nor the analysand can know what the "real" trouble is. In his view it is "there" but "indescribable." "An interpretation, we might say, provides a useful gloss on something that is, by definition, indescribable."[27] In spite of this lingering positivism (or possibly because of it), Spence's book received wide attention inside as well as outside psychoanalytic circles. It was widely interpreted to mean that the principal task of psychoanalysis and of "ego functioning" was the construction of a life story that fit the patient's present circumstances, and never mind whether it was "archaeologically true to memory" or not. Indeed, it was precisely in this spirit that David Polonoff picked up the debate a few years later, attempting to establish the claim that the "Self of a life" was a product of our narrative rather than some fixed but hidden "thing" that was its referent. The object of a self-narrative was not its fit to some hidden "reality" but its achievement of "external and internal *coherence, livability,* and *adequacy.*" Self-deception was a failure to achieve this, not a failure to correspond with an unspecifiable "reality."[28]

Roy Schafer took a more radical stance than Spence. For he was concerned not only, as it were, with the substance or content of constructed life-Selves, but also with their mode of construction. He says, for example:

> We are forever telling stories about ourselves. In telling these self-stories *to others* we may, for most purposes, be said to be performing straightforward narrative actions. In saying that we also tell them *to ourselves,* however, we are enclosing one story within another. This is the story that there is a self to tell something to, a someone else serving as audience who is one-

self or one's self. When the stories we tell others about ourselves concern these other selves of ours, when we say for example "I am not master of myself," we are again enclosing one story within another. On this view, the self is a telling. From time to time and from person to person this telling varies in the degree to which it is unified, stable, and acceptable to informed observers as reliable and valid.[29]

He goes on to note that *others* are also rendered narratively, so that our narrative about ourselves told to another is, in effect, "doubly narrative." "As a project in personal development, personal analysis changes the leading questions that one addresses to the tale of one's life and the lives of important others." The challenge to analyst and analysand then becomes, "let's see how we can retell it in a way that allows you to understand the origins, meanings, and significance of your present difficulties and to do so in a way that makes change conceivable and attainable."[30] And in the process, the analyst and analysand concentrate not only on the *content* but on the *form* of the narrative (Schafer calls it the "action" of the narrative) in which the *telling* itself is treated as the object to be described rather than being treated, so to speak, as a "transparent medium." The narrative's opaqueness, its circumstantiality, its genre, are taken to be as important as or, in any case, inseparable from its content. The analysand's Self, then, becomes not only a maker of tales, but one with a distinctive style. And under the circumstances, the analyst, it would seem, comes increasingly to serve in the role of helpful editor or provisional amanuensis. In any case, the analyst becomes complicit in the constructional process. And so begins a process through which a distributive Self is elaborated.

In much the same spirit, psychologists began to ask whether

the wider circle of people about whom any person cares or in whom he or she confides might also be complicit in our narratives and our Self-constructions. Might not the complicit circle, then, be something like a "distributed Self," much as one's notes and looking-up procedures become part of one's distributed knowledge. And just as knowledge thereby gets caught in the net of culture, so too Self becomes enmeshed in a net of others. It is this distributive picture of Self that came to prevail among "social constructionists" and "interpretive social scientists."[31]

The "narrative turn" had some surprising effects. It gave new punch to already lively disclaimers about the universality of the so-called Western conception of Selfhood, the view of "the person as a bounded, unique, more or less integrated motivational and cognitive universe, a dynamic center of awareness, emotion, judgment, and action, organized into a distinctive whole and set contrastively against such other wholes and against a social and natural background."[32] Though Self-as-strategic-reckoner is a view that can, in some fashion, make claim to universality by appealing to the universality of reason, universality is not so obvious when storytelling is invoked. Stories are many and varied; reason is governed by a compelling and single logic.

Once one takes a narrative view, one can ask why one story rather than another. And just such questioning soon led to the suspicion that "official" or "enforced" conceptions of Self might be used to establish political or hegemonic control by one group over another. Even within Western culture, a bustlingly active male view of Self may, in fact, marginalize women by making their Selves seem inferior. Feminist critics have written copiously in the last several years on the manner in which women's autobiography has been marginalized by the adoption of an all-male canon of autobiographical writing.[33]

Indeed, the "new" recognition that people narrativize their experience of the world and of their own role in it has even forced social scientists to reconsider how they use their principal instrument of research—the interview. The sociologist Elliot Mishler reminds us that in most interviews we expect respondents to answer our questions in the categorical form required in formal exchanges rather than in the narratives of natural conversation. We expect answers like "Meeting the financial strains" in response to "What were the hardest times early in your marriage?" As interviewers, we typically interrupt our respondents when they break into stories, or in any case we do not code the stories: they do not fit our conventional categories. So the human Selves that emerge from our interviews become artificialized by our interviewing method. Mishler illustrates the point with an interview where a respondent tells vividly what "paying his debts on time" meant to his self-esteem early in his marriage. He does so literally without ever answering the question about "hardest times in his marriage" at all.[34]

Perhaps the current state of play is most succinctly put by Donald Polkinghorne in his *Narrative Knowing and the Human Sciences*. Speaking of Self, he remarks:

> The tools being used by the human disciplines to gain access to the self-concept are, in general, the traditional research implements designed for formal science to locate and measure objects and things . . . We achieve our personal identities and self-concept through the use of the narrative configuration, and make our existence into a whole by understanding it as an

115

expression of a single unfolding and developing story. We are in the middle of our stories and cannot be sure how they will end; we are constantly having to revise the plot as new events are added to our lives. Self, then, is not a static thing or a substance, but a configuring of personal events into an historical unity which includes not only what one has been but also anticipations of what one will be.[35]

II   So what then of a cultural psychology of the kind I have been proposing? How would *it* go about posing the problem of the Self? Surely, the new developments just recounted would be congenial to it. It seems to me that a cultural psychology imposes two closely related requirements on the study of Self. One of them is that such studies must focus upon the *meanings* in terms of which Self is defined *both* by the individual *and* by the culture in which he or she participates. But this does not suffice if we are to understand how a "Self" is negotiated, for Self is not simply the resultant of contemplative reflection. The second requirement, then, is to attend to the *practices* in which "the meanings of Self" are achieved and put to use. These, in effect, provide us with a more "distributed" view of Self.

Let me consider each of these. We have already considered how *individuals* define their own Selves. By a *culture's* definition of Selfhood, part of my first requirement, I mean more than what contemporary Others, as it were, take as their working definition of Selves in general and of a particular Self (as in Gergen's interesting studies mentioned earlier). For there is a historical dimension as well. If Gergen's Self is "Self from the outside in," the historical Self is "Self from the past to the present." In our own culture, for example, views of Self are

116

shaped and buttressed by our Judeo-Christian theology and by the new Humanism that emerged in the Renaissance. They are shaped as well by a society, an economy, and a language, all of which have historical "realities" which, though open to revision, have created a scaffold that supports our practices as human agents. Our very conception of Selfhood is configured by the legal guarantees of its inviolability—as in *habeas corpus* and the Fourth Amendment to the U.S. Constitution, which carefully delineates our right to privacy. A cultural psychology that failed to take such matters into account would be perpetuating the antihistorical, anticultural bias that has created so much of the difficulty in contemporary psychology.[36]

Return now to the second criterion of a cultural psychology—that it explore not only meaning but its uses in practice. What could be meant by the "practice" of Self? *In practice* it was common at universities during the troubled late Sixties, for example, for students to request leave to go off and live for a term or a year in, say, a Vermont village or a cabin in the Maine woods in order to "get away from it all" so that they could "find themselves." These beliefs, desires, or reasons about Self and how to "find" it were as real to all involved as the college regulations that thwarted them, as real too as the psychic geography of those regions in which young people then thought they could find the "isolation" they sought. This was Self in use, its "meaning in praxis." It was Self distributed in action, in projects, in practice. You *went* to *somewhere* to *do something* with an anticipated *goal* in mind, something you couldn't do elsewhere and be the same Self. Moreover, you talked with others about it in a certain way. To be viable in a cultural psychology, concepts ("Self" included) must carry specification about how they are to be used both in action

117

and in the discourse that surrounds action. If I may use a literary example, it is like the young captain in Conrad's "The Secret Sharer" who must test his sense of autonomy by sailing his ship dangerously and skillfully close in off the dark and looming rock of Koh-ring so that Leggatt, the *Doppelgänger* whom the captain has hidden on board though he knows he was charged with the murder of a cowardly seaman on his own ship, can slip overboard and escape ashore, "a free man, a proud swimmer."[37] In the end, it is not the young captain's "autonomy" as a trait in isolation that matters in understanding his behavior, but how that sense of autonomy is narrativized into his life. And just as I commented two chapters back about the *interpretive* indeterminateness of Ibsen's three plays, so there is no ontologically *final* interpretation possible of the young captain's act. For there are no causes to be grasped with certainty where the act of creating meaning is concerned, only acts, expressions, and contexts to be interpreted. And that brings us to the heart of the matter.

A cultural psychology is an interpretive psychology, in much the sense that history and anthropology and linguistics are interpretive disciplines. But that does not mean that it need be unprincipled or without methods, even hard-nosed ones. It seeks out the rules that human beings bring to bear in creating meanings in cultural contexts. These contexts are always *contexts of practice:* it is always necessary to ask what people are *doing* or *trying* to do in that context. This is not a subtle point, that meaning grows out of use, but in spite of its being frequently sloganized, its implications are often unsuspected.

When is "Self" invoked, in what form, and to what end? Most people, to take a general case, do not regard gravity as

acting on their Selves (save perhaps in extreme cases). But if
somebody else grabs them or pushes them or forcibly takes
their purse, they will feel their Selves to have been "violated"
and will invoke Self in their description of what happened.
Agentivity is involved, their own and somebody else's. It is
much as I set it forth in the chapter on folk psychology. The
range of what people include as under the influence of their
own agentivity will, as we know from studies of "locus of
control," vary from person to person and, as we also know,
vary with one's felt position within the culture.[38] Moreover,
we feel some situations to be "impersonal," and in those situations we believe that our own Selves and the Selves of others
are not operative and not "legitimately" invocable. To get a
general notion of a particular "Self" in practice, we must sample its uses in a variety of contexts, culturally specifiable contexts.

In pursuit of this aim, we obviously cannot track people
through life and observe or interrogate them each step of the
way. Even if we could, doing so would transform the meaning
of what they were up to. And, in any case, we would not
know how to put the bits and pieces together at the end of the
inquiry. One viable alternative is obvious—to do the inquiry
retrospectively, through *autobiography*. And I do not mean an
autobiography in the sense of a "record" (for there is no such
thing). I mean, simply, an account of what one thinks one did
in what settings in what ways for what felt reasons. It will
inevitably be a narrative, as Polkinghorne remarked, and, to
pick up Schafer's point, its form will be as revealing as its
substance. It does not matter whether the account conforms
to what others might say who were witnesses, nor are we in
pursuit of such ontologically obscure issues as whether the

account is "self-deceptive" or "true." Our interest, rather, is only in what the person thought he did, what he thought he was doing it for, what kinds of plights he thought he was in, and so on.

III Let me demonstrate all too briefly how one can go about such a study of Self with requisite interpretive rigor. I must begin somewhat autobiographically. Some years ago, my colleagues and I became interested in the nature of narrative as text and as mode of thought. Like others, we had concentrated on how people reproduced stories whose texts were available for comparison. Eventually, and naturally, we became interested in how people would tell stories on their own, quite apart from what they had heard. Thinking that their own lives might provide a good material for such telling, we set out to collect a few spontaneous autobiographies. We let each subject be guided by what Philippe Lejeune calls "a rough draft, perpetually reshaped, of the story of his life," and very soon we discovered that we were listening to people in the act of *constructing* a longitudinal version of Self.[39] What we were observing was by no means a "free" construction. It was constrained by the events of a life, to be sure, but it was also powerfully constrained by the demands of the story the teller was in process of constructing. It was inevitably a story of development, but the forms that it took (while recognizably cultural in their form) were far more varied than we had ever expected.

As stories of development, these "spontaneous autobiographies" were constituted of smaller stories (of events, happenings, projects), each of which achieved its significance by virtue of being part of a larger-scale "life." In this respect they shared a universal feature of all narratives. The larger overall narratives were told in easily recognizable genres—the tale of a victim, a *Bildungsroman,* antihero forms, *Wanderung* stories, black comedy, and so on. The storied events that they comprised made sense only in terms of the larger picture. At the center of each account dwelled a protagonist Self in process of construction: whether active agent, passive experiencer, or vehicle of some ill-defined destiny. And at critical junctures, "turning points" emerged, again culturally recognizable, produced almost invariably by an access of new consciousness aroused by victory or defeat, by betrayal of trust, and so on. It soon became apparent not only that life imitated art but that it did so by choosing art's genres and its other devices of storytelling as its modes of expression.

There is something curious about autobiography. It is an account given by a narrator in the here and now about a protagonist bearing his name who existed in the there and then, the story terminating in the present when the protagonist fuses with the narrator. The narrative episodes that compose the life story are typically Labovian in structure, with strict adherence to sequence and to justification by exceptionality. But the larger story reveals a strong rhetorical strand, as if justifying why it was necessary (*not* causally, but morally, socially, psychologically) that the life had gone a particular way. The Self as narrator not only recounts but justifies. And the Self as protagonist is always, as it were, pointing to the future. When somebody says, as if summing up a childhood, "I was a pretty rebellious kid," it can usually be taken as a prophecy as much as a summary.

There is an enormous amount of work going on here and

now as the story is being put together. Not surprising, then, that in the dozens of autobiographies we have collected and analyzed, between a third and a half of the "nuclear propositions" are in the present tense—the narrator not telling about the past, which is almost always told in the past tense, but deciding what to make of the past narratively at the moment of telling.

The presuppositions that we lace into the telling of our lives are deep and virtually limitless. They are in every line: "modest childhood," "dreamy kid," and so on. And why things are included remains mostly implicit, the unspoken pact in force being that you, the mostly listening interviewer, will figure that out for yourself. And if you should ask that reasons be made explicit, your question will surely steer the account in a direction that it would have not taken otherwise. For the interviewer becomes part of that "swarm of participations" that distributes Self across its occasions of use.

This dense undergrowth of presupposition in autobiography made our task difficult, but in reaction we hit upon a few happy defensive ideas. The best of them was to concentrate upon members of the same family. That way we would have a better sense of what it meant when one member said "We were a close family." But that pragmatic decision brought other gifts that we could never have foreseen. A family, after all, is (as writers on the subject are fond of putting it) the vicar of the culture and, as well, a microcosm of it. So rather than continuing to collect autobiographies from isolated individuals, we decided to concentrate on six members of the same family. What started as a matter of convenience ended as a principle of research.

And so the Goodhertzes: mother and father in their early

sixties with two grown sons and two grown daughters. We interviewed them individually and independently about their lives, spent a year doing a preliminary analysis of their individual autobiographies, and then brought them back together as a family for a "discussion session," lasting more than three hours, to talk about "what it's like growing up a Goodhertz." Fortunately, we videotaped that session, for families without their gestures and some indication of whom they are looking at are like sunsets without color.

We also thought we could dig out presuppositions buried in the life stories by a close study of the language used in them. A narrative, after all, is not just a plot, a *fabula*, but a way of telling, a *sjuzet*. So we analyzed the discourse itself, finding the revealing words, the signature expressions, the telltale grammatical forms. And we counted deontic and epistemic modals to see how much each member of the family leaned on contingency and necessity in putting structure into their accounts. We examined the contexts of use of mental verbs to enrich our picture of Goodhertz subjectivity. Fortunately, counts and specific searches can easily be done by computer. But hints about how to interpret them are something else again. There, our best guide was literary and discourse linguistics.

IV   Our interviewing procedure was informal, and designed to encourage meaning-making by narrative recounting rather than the more categorical responses one obtains in standard interviews. We explained at the start of each interview that we were interested in spontaneous autobiography and in how people go about telling their lives, in their own ways.[40]

We—my colleague Susan Weisser, a professor of English literature, and I—made known our longtime interest in the topic
and made plain that we were not interested in making judgments or in doing therapy, that we were interested in "lives."
Then Dr. Weisser conducted each interview in her office on
her own over a period of several months.

Despite the epistemological burdens that modern theorists
of autobiography have discussed over the last fifteen years,
ordinary people, or even extraordinary ones, once into the
task, have little difficulty with telling their stories. No doubt
the stories we heard were designed in some measure for our
interest in how people tell about their lives. Nor were we
under any illusion that an interviewer could be neutral during
the interviews: Dr. Weisser laughed when something funny
was told, responded appropriately to events recounted with
the usual "hmms" and "Goodness me's," and even asked for
clarification when something said was genuinely unclear to
her. For her to have done otherwise would surely have violated the rules of ordinary dialogue. Dr. Weisser is a woman
in her forties, warm and informally friendly, quite evidently
fascinated both personally and professionally by "lives," and
she acted in character. Our subjects obviously responded in a
fashion that reflected her "appreciative" style and, no doubt,
would have reacted differently to an interviewer who was, say,
more "formal" or whose persona was different in some other
way or, simply, who was a man rather than a woman. Indeed,
an elaborate research study can (and should) be generated
around issues of this order, but we decided that such a project
was not an appropriate one for a first venture. Obviously,
"the-story-of-a-life" as told to a particular person is in some
deep sense a joint product of the teller and the told. Selves,

whatever metaphysical stand one takes about the "reality," can only be revealed in a transaction between a teller and a told, and as Mishler reminds us, whatever topic one approaches by interviewing must be evaluated in the light of that transaction.[41] That much said, all that one can counsel is the exercise of a certain interpretive caution.

We made up a list of a dozen "prompt questions" to ask when subjects had come to the end of their first spontaneous account, from a quarter-hour to an hour into the interview—questions always put in the same order. They ranged from initially very open-ended ones, like "How would you say your parents regarded you as a child?" to such later prompting queries as "Was there anything in your life that you would say was quite untypical of you?" or "If you had to describe your life as a novel or a play or a story, what would you say it was most like?" The interviews lasted from an hour to nearly two hours and were, of course, recorded. All six of the Goodhertzes, in one context or another, later remarked spontaneously that they had enjoyed the interview and/or that they had found it personally very informative. Several said that they had been quite surprised by what came out. This last, by the way, is very common in autobiographical interviewing and speaks in an interesting way to the constructional nature of "telling about your life."

As for the "family session," I began it by telling them we had been studying their autobiographies and were now fascinated to hear their views of what it was like to grow up a Goodhertz. The session went on for three hours without there being any occasion for us to introduce any of the prompts that we had cautiously designed just in case. It was still going strong when we ended it, having decided in advance that three hours was enough. We met around a seminar table, with coffee and refreshments available. It was not an interview, though certainly the Goodhertzes were always aware of our presence and in some sense speaking to us even if they seemed to be addressing their comments to one another as often as to us. Indeed there were times when we, the investigators, seemed to be ignored altogether.

We knew that they were a "close" family who boasted of their freedom to "discuss anything and everything" as a family. And they were sufficiently unselfconscious that their conversation around the table even took some confrontational turns, particularly on intergenerational issues. At one point, Debby, the youngest daughter, in her mid-twenties but still considered "the baby of the family," attacked her parents as "racist," for their attitudes toward a Black former boyfriend. Her mother replied that if God had intended for the races to mix, He would not have made them in different colors. Like anybody invested in keeping an atmosphere congenial I took advantage of the pause that ensued to announce that a new pot of coffee had arrived. I realized only later that I was "behaving family." For as Clifford Geertz had counseled me when we were starting, families are systems for keeping people from being pulled centrifugally by inevitably conflicting interests, and this family had two techniques for doing so. One was by adroit interpersonal management: joking, diversion, and the rest—as in my "coffee" announcement. The other was by falling into and playing established family roles, even to the use of canonical family stories that serve to highlight those roles. Every family has a store of these, and this one uses them deftly, as we shall see presently.

V   Let me give you a very quick sketch of the Goodhertz family, enough so that what follows will be comprehensible. George Goodhertz heads the family: a self-made man in his sixties, a heating contractor dedicated to work but just as proud of his role as a trusted man in the community to whom friends turn in trouble, whether for advice or for small loans. His father, by his testimony, was "a drinker" and a poor provider, and when he deserted the family, George was taken into a parochial school without fees. He tells us that he became a favorite of the nuns, who responded to his eagerness to help around the place. He became a Catholic, the family before then having had only a vague Protestant connection. He says he is no longer a believer, though he is keenly conscious of the moral obligations he learned in the church and tries to live by them. He is a reflective man, though he never finished high school, and the language of his autobiography contains a high density of words or phrases differentiating what "seems to be" from what "is." He is effective and self-contained, but worries that he has missed intimacy in his life. By falsifying his birthday, he joined the army underage, and left five years later, still under twenty-five, as a master sergeant. But he does not think of himself in any sense as a tough guy, though he's convinced you have to be "street smart" to make out in this world.

Rose, his wife, is a second-generation Italian-American, very family oriented, much involved with old friends in the Brooklyn neighborhood where they've lived for thirty years, "a Catholic and a Democrat." Like her husband, she is the child of a father who, in her words, was "of the old school":

a boaster, a drinker, a poor provider, and unfaithful. The two of them, husband and wife, share a dedication to giving their children a better life than they themselves had. She enjoys her reputation in the family as stubborn. When the children were grown she "went back to work"—bookkeeper for her husband, but for pay. Not as reflective as her husband, she has a strong belief in fate, a fate that can be influenced by one's own efforts, as in "with the help of fate, I raised my children so that none of them was ever on drugs." The transcript of her autobiographical interview is full of the language of indicative realism, and low in efforts to "interpret meaning." "Is" takes pride of place over "seems."

The eldest child, Carl, active in the Catholic Peace Movement as a high school student, is the first in the family to have gone to college—to a Catholic college, upon graduation from which he went on to take his Ph.D. in sensory physiology from a decidedly secular university "out of town." He is reflective, sequential, and didactic in his autobiographical account, the spirit of it caught by such expressions as "had I known then what I know now." Aware of how far he has gone beyond the family in his education, he still keeps close contact with them. But he says toward the end of his autobiography, Icarus-like and only half self-mocking, "What's a boy from Brooklyn doing way up here?" He believes in his "specialness," a specialness that allows him to see through cant and hypocrisy and to go his own way. He is the natural ally of his sister Debby, the least linear, and most spontaneous in the family. He is unmarried in his latter thirties, lives in Manhattan where he works at a research job, but is usually home for Sunday dinners in Brooklyn.

Nina is the next in line. An obedient, fat child by her testimony, she says she became more rebellious when her father disapproved of her lively dressing and outgoingness. "I was supposed to wear blacks and browns and be quiet." She soon married a man who became alcoholic, had a daughter by him, separated, and moved back home. Then she discovered entrepreneurship, successfully selling homemade chocolates to local stores. Her life changed, she tells us. Armed with a new confidence, she got a job marketing a telephone answering service, soon after got into her own service, and is now doing very well. Asked at the end of her autobiographical interview what she would most like out of life, she answered laughingly, "More." Nina laughs easily, and uses her laughter to help her parents and siblings over tense places. Her laughing effort at reconciliation can be overheard in the background during Debby's confrontation with her parents over racism. Whether feigned or genuine, self-mockery is one of her ways of endearing herself to her family. At the time of the family session she had been remarried and divorced again in the year since we had seen her, and she announced this to us in her "jolly large woman" self-mocking way with, "I guess marriage is my hobby now." For all her entrepreneurship, she is very strongly identified with her family and her daughter and sees herself as in her mother's mold.

Harry is the bad-luck story in the family. He tried hardest to please, but was plainly not a happy child. He over-ate so excessively as a small child that, as told in one of those canonical family stories, his mother put a DO NOT FEED sign around his neck when he went out into the neighborhood. Harry's autobiographical narrative is somehow dysphasic. He is poor at preserving the order of events, his intentions come across unclearly, and he is confusingly exophoric in reference in the sense that the text does not always reveal what he is referring to. He married a local girl when he was quite young, and to make her feel more "at home" he encouraged her to see her old friends, including an old boyfriend, and this caused trouble. In time, she "stole" the money he had collected from his bowling club. He "roughed her up" for that, he tells us. They had a child, divorced shortly after, and it is not clear from his report how she managed to do him out of visitation rights. In any case, while under all this stress, he blew up at a customer while on his city job and was dismissed or suspended. When he told us his story, he was involved in two lawsuits: one to get the right to visit his son, the other to get his job back. Life was on hold. His account had the largest proportion of incomplete, nonparsable sentences of any of them, and the least structured narrative. In a most touching way, both in interviews and in the family session, there was real deference and caring for Harry. "I think he's the nicest one of all of us," his mother said.

Debby had the indulged childhood, she said, of the youngest in the family—youngest by several years. She had many friends in the neighborhood, was much liked, and then went to a local college where she hated the anonymity. Personalness is what she cares most about, personalness but not of a kind that gets you stuck in the old routines of the neighborhood—"just getting married and ending up cooped up by four walls with four kids." She wants "experience," wants to know the world. Her ideal is "spontaneity" and "lightness." She has chosen to go into acting and is now in drama school. Working on new roles, she says, is what excites her. Her autobiography is a succession of vividly described impressions, put together as a set of variations on the themes of experience, intimacy, and spontaneity. In what one reader of her account called her "postmodern style," she is as orderly as Carl in the sense of relating themes to one another, but while his is a causal, linear account, hers is a metaphorically linked flow of themes, blending one into the other. Causal expressions are relatively rare, but their lack is made up for by a vividness and concreteness of evocative detail. She is accepted in the family for what she is: warm, spontaneous, loyal to her family, but deficient in "street smarts." She cares about being an actress, but her ambition seems more personal than worldly.

Every face-to-face culture has its occasions of "joint attention" where members come together to "catch up" on the state of things, to recalibrate their feelings toward one another, and, as it were, to reaffirm the canon. Families are no exception: Thanksgiving or Christmas dinners, Passover Seders, weddings, and so on. The Goodhertzes' "closeness," they felt, was based on having meals together often. They lived within easy reach of one another (save for Carl) and "sat around the table together," to use their phrase, at least once a week. They boasted that nothing was barred around that table. And they had been sitting around it since the children were small. There was also an unwritten rule that you could return home in trouble and reclaim your old room. Nina returned there with her daughter after her divorces; so did Harry after his unhappy breakup. At the time of her autobiographical interview, Debby was still living there. When later she moved out to be nearer her drama school in another part of Brooklyn, her sister teased her good-naturedly about bringing her laundry back home for washing.

VI   Let me now return to the issue that I initially set out to address: the shaping and distribution of Self in the practices of a family, with the family acting as the vicar of the culture. I shall only be able to deal with one theme—the distinction that all the Goodhertzes make between public and private, a cultural distinction that finds its way from the outside society into a family's ideology and is finally embodied in the Selves of its members. My object is not so much to "report" findings as to give a sense of how research can be conducted in the spirit of cultural psychology.

As you will doubtless have gathered, the contrast between "home" and (to use Goodhertz language) "the real world" is central to this family and to each member of it. Of the "themes" discussed in both the autobiographies and the family session, this is the dominant one. It leads in frequency of mention, it is entailed most often in the resolution of imbalances in the Burkean pentad that comprise the "stories" they tell, and it is the issue most likely to create what in an earlier chapter I referred to as "Trouble" with a capital T. It is also the theme that generates the highest frequency of deontic propositions—statements about what *should* be, what can be counted upon, what one is obliged to take into account.

The distinction has taken many forms in different eras. Its expression in this family is a contemporary expression. For the Goodhertz autobiographical texts are, as it were, as much historical and sociological documents as they are personal ones. Indeed, this family's "personal" history even reflects in some profound way the history of immigration in America—of immigrants from Italy to America on one side of the family, and from upstate to the city on the other. George and Rose

Goodhertz both lived through childhoods that, in their own words, were marred by near-poverty and its mean consequences. Both were so eager to guard their children from such a childhood that, without intending to do so, they exaggerated the contrast between "home" and "real world" to a point where it created tension for the children—tension about "safe versus dangerous" and about "boring versus exciting." Both parents stressed that their deepest wish was to "spare" their children a childhood like theirs.

But there is also a sociological truth of the matter, where the distinction is concerned. Contemporary New Yorkers *see* and *talk about* their city as crime-ridden, drug-ridden, notably incivil, exploitative, and, at the same time, exciting and innovative. The very expression "street smarts" is New Yorkese, an invitation to distinguish between public and private in a particular way. It expresses both history and sociology, as well as individual psychology. Cultural psychology, obviously, is not bent on "confusing" the different levels of analysis represented by these three fields, each with its necessarily different data bases. Yet one of its principal aims is to explore the manner in which each provides a context for the others.

"Home" for the Goodhertzes is intimacy, trust, mutual aid, forgiveness, openness. It is a prescription for commitment, a way of relating to others, a mode of discourse, even a kind of affect. As one would expect, it is also embodied in emblematic stories that family members tell about "the family," narratives that illustrate symbolic plights and symbolic resolutions (or amusing nonresolutions). Each member has his or her own stories to tell. Debby, for example, specializes in ones about helplessness, even "dumb animal helplessness," as unlocking Goodhertz family sympathy. There is "her" story of the wing-broke seagull, alighting helplessly in the Goodhertz yard, whose exaggerated pampering by the family until he dies is told years after as an absurdist exaggeration of what "soft touches" they all are. She told it at the family meeting; they all embroidered. Or there is her autobiographical account of the chicken fallen from a truck on the Brooklyn-Queens Expressway, with a narrative twist symbolizing her grownup allegiance to the same ideal. Her friend refuses to stop the car for her to rescue it: "We'll all be killed." She fumes: the "real world," the horrendous BQE, has canceled human kindness.

Carl's "real world" is more deliberate in its cruelty and hypocrisy, more corrupt than Debby's. He is told by the high school football coach to "get" an opposing end, "get him out of the game." He quits the team altogether—quietly and with no fanfare. He adjusts to his version of the "real world" by finding like-minded, sympathetic enclaves in it—the Catholic Peace Movement, a settlement house where he gave his free time as a college student. In graduate school, rather than be put off by "cutthroat competition," and "faculty separateness," he tries to get things so that "we can all sit down and talk about things like equals"—the key metaphor of the family at home. In his stories, "standing up" to the pressures requires something special. "We're a moral family," he announced at the family session, quite out of the blue.

Each has his or her own narrative version of the conflict, even the reserved Mr. Goodhertz recounting his tale of intimacy thwarted by his demands for trustworthiness and confidentiality from friends. Or another confrontation at the family session, one plainly on the way to becoming a "story." Debby blasts her father for not having shown more sympathy when, some months before, she told him on the phone of the death of a friend. He says, "Look, I really didn't know her. In this world you can't be torn apart by everything." He knows he is treading perilously close to the bristling frontier between fatherly intimacy and real-world street smarts. After all, as a hard-hat true-blue patriot and former master sergeant, he gave Carl his blessing as a Vietnam draft evader. And Debby keeps returning to the theme of "losing herself," by which she means getting overly involved in her career.

All of which is not to say that the Goodhertzes have given up ambitions in the "real world." They have not. But to a striking degree, their feelings of self-legitimacy derive not from "succeeding out there" but from their identification with and participation in the "home" world of trust and intimacy. And in this sense, this family surely mirrors what many writers refer to as the contemporary "privatization" of meaning and of Self. In the family sessions as in the autobiographies, there is little question that, as they depict it, the "real Self" is not the "outside persona" but the feelings and beliefs attached to the values of privacy, intimacy, mutual exchange. The Good-hertz Selves, if I may use an emblematic metaphor, are distrib-uted around that famous dinner table. When Dr. Weisser and I were vaguely invited by Mrs. Goodhertz to have an Italian dinner with them at home, we took it for the semiotic act that it was: *we* had become real people too, resident selves of the world that is "home."

The prime structure of Self in each of the Goodhertzes is just this division between the legitimizing "real Self" and the instrumental "street-smart" Self that protects them from the "real world." The two are in an uneasy balance with each other. A story from Carl's autobiography provides a poignant illustration. In California for the summer, he meets a girl with whom he has an affair. "A lotus eater" is how he describes her. She tells him one evening, chatting in bed, to stop driving himself so hard. Next morning early he gets up, gathers his things, takes the first plane back to New York—all before she wakens. It is not *dolce far niente* that he wants, but the comforting discomfort of living with his self-defining conflict.

VII   Now we must return to a historical perspective. We forget at our peril as psychologists that, as recently as the eighteenth century, the private domain was not so real, not so self-defining, not so stabilizing as the public world of work and power. As the English historian Keith Thomas reminds us in his thoughtful review of the third volume of the *Annales* school's *A History of Private Life*:

> In later periods of European history, privacy was equated with secrecy, concealment, and a shameful desire to shelter from the gaze of the community. As one seventeenth-century preacher put it, "The murderer and the adulterer are alike desirous of privacy." In the eighteenth century Denis Diderot saw the proliferation of furniture containing secret compartments as a sign of the age's moral deterioration . . . For Jean-Jacques Rousseau, a society with no privacy would be a society with no vice.[42]

The lives and Selves we have been exploring are, to be sure, shaped by intrapsychic forces operating in the here and now. The distinction that they share, the sharp difference between Home and the Real World, is *their* distinction, and they have appropriated it into their own lives. It is in every sense vibrantly *contemporary*. But to let the matter rest at that is to rob the Goodhertzes of history and to impoverish our own understanding of their lives and their plight. For individually and as a family they are, always have been, and can never escape being expressions of social and historical forces. Whatever constituted those "forces," whatever view one may take of historical forces, they were converted into human meanings, into language, into narratives, and found their way into the minds of men and women. In the end, it was this conversion process that created folk psychology and the *experienced* world of culture.

A cultural psychology takes these matters as its domain. It does not do so, as I have been at pains to repeat more than a few times, by ruling out or by denying the existence of biological limits and physical and even economic necessities. On the other hand, it insists that the "methodology of causation" can neither capture the social and personal richness of lives in a culture nor begin to plumb their historical depth. It is only through the application of interpretation that we, as psychologists, can do justice to the world of culture.

VIII   Let me draw these four chapters to a conclusion. I began by decrying the Cognitive Revolution for abandoning "meaning-making" as its central concern, opting for "information processing" and computation instead. In the second chapter I urged that we take into account in our studies of the human condition what I called "folk psychology," the culturally shaped notions in terms of which people organize their views of themselves, of others, and of the world in which they live. Folk psychology, I insisted, is an essential base not only of personal meaning but of cultural cohesion. For it is in support of its tenets that we create our institutions, with folk psychology changing, in its turn, in response to institutional change. I also tried to make clear that folk psychology is not so much a set of logical propositions as it is an exercise in narrative and storytelling. It is supported by a powerful structure of narrative culture—stories, myths, genres of literature.

In the third chapter, I explored the origins of this readiness to participate in human culture and to use its narratives. I tried to indicate how the young, by native endowment and by exposure, came to participate in culture by *using* language and its narrative discourse *in vivo*. I even speculated that the structure of human grammar might have arisen out of proto-linguistic push to narrate.

Finally, I have tried to show how the lives and Selves we construct are the outcomes of this process of meaning-construction. But I have also tried to make it clear that Selves are not isolated nuclei of consciousness locked in the head, but are "distributed" interpersonally. Nor do Selves arise rootlessly in response only to the present; they take meaning as well from the historical circumstances that gave shape to the culture of which they are an expression.

The program of a cultural psychology is not to deny biology or economics, but to show how human minds and lives are reflections of culture and history as well as of biology and physical resources. Necessarily, it uses the tools of interpretation that have always served the student of culture and history. There is no one "explanation" of man, biological or otherwise. In the end, even the strongest causal explanations of the human condition cannot make plausible sense without being interpreted in the light of the symbolic world that constitutes human culture.

Notes

Index

Notes

1. The Proper Study of Man

1. Howard Gardner, *The Mind's New Science: A History of the Cognitive Revolution* (New York: Basic Books, 1985). Earl Hunt, "Cognitive Science: Definition, Status, and Questions," *Annual Review of Psychology* 40 (1989):603–629.
2. Hubert L. Dreyfus and Stuart E. Dreyfus, with Tom Athanasiou, *Mind over Machine: The Power of Human Intuition and Expertise in the Era of the Computer* (New York: Free Press, 1986). Terry Winograd, *Understanding Computers and Cognition: A New Foundation for Design* (Reading, Mass.: Addison-Wesley, 1987).
3. Clifford Geertz, *The Interpretation of Cultures* (New York: Basic Books, 1973). Clifford Geertz, *Local Knowledge: Further Essays in Intepretive Anthropology* (New York: Basic Books, 1983). George Lakoff and Mark Johnson, *Metaphors We Live By* (Chicago: University of Chicago Press, 1980). John R. Searle, *Intentionality: An Essay in the Philosophy of Mind* (New York: Cambridge University Press, 1983). Nelson Goodman, *Of Mind and Other Matters* (Cambridge, Mass.: Harvard University Press, 1984). Wolfgang Iser, *The Act of Reading: A Theory of Aesthetic Response* (Baltimore: Johns Hopkins University Press, 1978). Kenneth J. Gergen, *Toward Transformation in Social Knowledge*

141

(New York: Springer-Verlag, 1982). Kenneth J. Gergen and Keith E. Davis, *The Social Construction of the Person* (New York: Springer-Verlag, 1985). Donald P. Spence, *Narrative Truth and Historical Truth: Meaning and Interpretation in Psychoanalysis* (New York: W. W. Norton, 1982). Donald E. Polkinghorne, *Narrative Knowing and the Human Sciences* (Albany: SUNY Press, 1988).

4. Edward C. Tolman, "Cognitive Maps in Rats and Men," *Psychological Review* 55 (1948):189–208. Tolman, *Purposive Behavior in Animals and Men* (New York: Century, 1932).

5. *Annual Reports of the Harvard University Center for Cognitive Studies* (Cambridge, Mass., 1961–1969).

6. George A. Miller, personal communication.

7. See, for example, Roy Lachman, Janet L. Lachman, and Earl C. Butterfield, *Cognitive Psychology and Information Processing: An Introduction* (Hillsdale, N.J.: Lawrence Erlbaum Associates, 1979).

8. Herbert A. Simon, *The Sciences of the Artificial,* 2nd ed. (Cambridge, Mass.: MIT Press, 1981).

9. Daniel C. Dennett, "Evolution of Consciousness," The Jacobsen Lecture, University of London, May 13, 1988; Alan M. Turing, "Computing Machinery and Intelligence," *Mind* 59 (1950):433–460.

10. Compare Noam Chomsky, *Language and the Problems of Knowledge: The Managua Lectures* (Cambridge, Mass.: MIT Press, 1988), with David E. Rumelhart, James L. McClelland, and the PDP Research Group, *Parallel Distributed Processing: Explorations in the Microstructure of Cognition,* vol. 1: *Foundations* (Cambridge, Mass.: MIT Press, 1986). James L. McClelland, David E. Rumelhart, and the PDP Research Group, *Parallel Distributed Processing: Explorations in the Microstructure of Cognition,* vol. 2: *Psychological and Biological Models* (Cambridge, Mass.: MIT Press, 1986).

11. Stephen P. Stich, *From Folk Psychology to Cognitive Science: The Case against Belief* (Cambridge, Mass.: MIT Press, 1983).

12. Daniel C. Dennett, *The Intentional Stance* (Cambridge, Mass.: MIT Press, 1987).

13. Paul M. Churchland, "The Ontological Status of Intentional States: Nailing Folk Psychology to Its Porch," *Behavioral and Brain Sciences* 11 (1988):507–508.

14. Jerry A. Fodor, *The Language of Thought* (New York: Crowell, 1975). Fodor, *Psychosemantics: The Problem of Meaning in the Philosophy of Mind* (Cambridge, Mass.: MIT Press, 1987).

15. Dennett, *Intentional Stance.*

16. Charles Taylor, *Sources of the Self* (Cambridge, Mass.: Harvard University Press, 1989). And see note 3 above.

17. Lev S. Vygotsky, *Thought and Language* (Cambridge, Mass.: MIT Press, 1962).

18. Geertz, *Interpretation of Cultures,* p. 49.

19. Ibid.

20. John L. Austin, "A Plea for Excuses," in Austin, *Philosophical Papers,* 2nd ed. (Oxford: Clarendon Press, 1970), 175–204.

21. Thomas Nagel, *The View from Nowhere* (New York: Oxford University Press, 1986).

22. Richard Rorty, *Philosophy and the Mirror of Nature* (Princeton: Princeton University Press, 1979).

23. Paul Ricoeur, *Freud and Philosophy: An Essay on Interpretation,* trans. Denis Savage (New Haven: Yale University Press, 1970).

24. Richard E. Nisbett and Lee Ross, *Human Inference: Strategies and Shortcomings of Social Judgment* (Englewood Cliffs, N.J.: Prentice-Hall, 1980).

25. Daniel Kahnemann, Paul Slovic, and Amos Tversky, *Judgment under Uncertainty: Heuristics and Biases* (New York: Cambridge University Press, 1982). Jerome S. Bruner, Jacqueline J. Goodnow, and George A. Austin, *A Study of Thinking* (New York: John Wiley and Sons, 1956).

26. John L. Austin, *How to Do Things with Words* (Cambridge, Mass.: Harvard University Press, 1962).

27. For a particularly searching and well-informed view of this same terrain, see Michael Cole, "Cultural Psychology," in *Nebraska Symposium: 1989* (Lincoln: University of Nebraska Press, forthcoming).

28. G. A. Miller, "The Magical Number Seven, Plus or Minus Two: Some Limits on Our Capacity for Processing Information," *Psychological Review* 63 (1956):81–97.

29. Elaine Scarry, *The Body in Pain: The Making and Unmaking of the World* (New York: Oxford University Press, 1985).

30. Hans Peter Rickman, *Wilhelm Dilthey: Pioneer of the Human Studies* (Berkeley: University of California Press, 1979). Wilhelm Dilthey, *Descriptive Psychology and Historical Understanding* (1911), trans. Richard M. Zaner and Kenneth L. Heiges (The Hague: Nijhoff, 1977).

31. See Goodman, *Of Mind and Other Matters,* for a well-argued statement of the philosophical foundations of this position.

32. Carol Fleisher Feldman, "Thought from Language: The Linguistic Construction of Cognitive Representations," in Jerome Bruner and Helen Haste, eds., *Making Sense: The Child's Construction of the World* (London: Methuen, 1987).

33. Richard Rorty, *Consequences of Pragmatism: Essays, 1972–1980* (Minneapolis: University of Minnesota Press, 1982).

34. Richard Rorty, "Pragmatism, Relativism, and Irrationalism," in *Consequences of Pragmatism.* Quotations from p. 162ff.

35. Howard Gardner, *Frames of Mind: The Theory of Multiple Intelligences* (New York: Basic Books, 1983).

36. James Clifford, *The Predicament of Culture: Twentieth-Century Ethnography, Literature, and Art* (Cambridge, Mass.: Harvard University Press, 1988).

37. See, for example, Sandor Ferenczi, *Thalassa: A Theory of Genitality,* trans. Henry A. Bunker (New York: W. W. Norton, 1968).

38. See Debra Friedman and Michael Hechter, "The Contribution of Rational Choice Theory to Macrosociological Research," *Sociological Theory* 6 (1988):201–218, for a discussion of the applicability of rational choice theory to social decision making generally.

39. I am indebted to Richard Herrnstein for providing this particular example of a "rational anomaly."

40. Taylor, *Sources of the Self.*

41. Edward Sapir, "Culture, Genuine and Spurious," in *Culture, Language and Personality: Selected Essays,* ed. David G. Mandelbaum (Berkeley: University of California Press, 1956), 78–119.

42. B. F. Skinner, *Beyond Freedom and Dignity* (New York: Alfred A. Knopf, 1972).

43. Wolfgang Kohler, *The Place of Value in a World of Facts* (New York: Liveright, 1938).

44. J. Kirk T. Varnedoe, "Introduction," in Varnedoe, ed., *Modern Portraits: The Self and Others* (New York: Columbia University, Department of Art History and Archaeology, 1976).

45. Adrienne Rich, "Invisibility in Academe," quoted in Renato Rosaldo, *Culture and Truth: The Remaking of Social Analysis* (Boston: Beacon Press, 1989), ix.

2. Folk Psychology as an Instrument of Culture

1. Gerald M. Edelman, *Neural Darwinism: The Theory of Neuronal Group Selection* (New York: Basic Books, 1987). Gerald M. Edelman, *The Remembered Present: A Biological Theory of Consciousness* (New York: Basic Books, 1990). Vernon Reynolds, *The Biology of Human Action,* 2nd ed. (San Francisco: W. H. Freeman, 1980). Roger Lewin, *Human Evolution: An Illustrated Introduction,* 2nd ed. (Boston: Blackwell Scientific Publications, 1989). Nicholas Humphrey, *The Inner Eye* (Boston: Faber and Faber, 1986).

2. Hans Peter Rickman, *Wilhelm Dilthey: Pioneer of the Human Studies* (Berkeley: University of California Press, 1979). Wilhelm Dilthey, *Descriptive Psychology and Historical Understanding* (1911), trans. Richard M. Zaner and Kenneth L. Heiges (The Hague: Nijhoff, 1977).

3. Stephen P. Stich, *From Folk Psychology to Cognitive Science: The Case against Belief* (Cambridge, Mass.: MIT Press, 1983).

4. Claude Lévi-Strauss, *The Savage Mind* (Chicago: University of Chicago Press, 1966). C. O. Frake, "The Diagnosis of Disease among the Subanun of Mindanao," *American Anthropology* 63; rpt. in D. Hymes, ed., *Language in Culture and Society* (New York: Harper and Row, 1964), 193–206. Thomas Gladwin, *East Is a Big Bird: Navigation and Logic on Puluwat Atoll* (Cambridge, Mass.: Harvard University Press, 1970). Edwin Hutchins, "Understanding Micronesian Navigation," in Dedre Gentner and Albert L. Stevens, eds., *Mental Models* (Hillsdale, N.J.: Lawrence Erlbaum Associates, 1983), 191–226.

5. Meyer Fortes, "Social and Psychological Aspects of Education in Taleland," *Africa* 11, no. (1938), supplement. Margaret Mead, *Coming of Age in Samoa* (New York: Morrow, 1928).

6. E. E. Evans-Pritchard, *Nuer Religion* (New York: Oxford University Press, 1974).

7. Harold Garfinkel, *Studies in Ethnomethodology* (Englewood Cliffs, N.J.: Prentice-Hall, 1967). Garfinkel, ed., *Ethnomethodological Studies of Work* (London and New York: Routledge and Kegan Paul, 1986). Fritz Heider, *The Psychology of Interpersonal Relations* (New York: John Wiley and Sons, 1958). Alfred Schutz, *The Problem of Social Reality*, ed. M. Natanson (The Hague: Nijhoff, 1962). Schutz, *On Phenomenology and Social Relations: Selected Writings of Alfred Schutz*, ed. Helmut R. Wagner (Chicago: University of Chicago Press, 1970). A more contemporary, anthropologically oriented view of these matters is presented by Richard A. Shweder, "Cultural Psychology: What Is It?" in J. W. Stigler, R. A. Shweder, and G. Herdt,

eds., *Cultural Psychology: The Chicago Symposium on Culture and Human Development* (New York: Cambridge University Press, 1989).

8. B. F. Skinner, *Beyond Freedom and Dignity* (New York: Alfred A. Knopf, 1972). Stich, *From Folk Psychology to Cognitive Science.*

9. Charles Taylor, *Sources of the Self* (Cambridge, Mass.: Harvard University Press, 1989).

10. André Gide, *Lafcadio's Adventure* (New York: Random House, 1925).

11. Daniel C. Dennett and John C. Haugeland, "Intentionality," in Richard L. Gregory, ed., *The Oxford Companion to the Mind* (Oxford and New York: Oxford University Press, 1987), 383–386.

12. Gladwin, *East Is a Big Bird.*

13. Michelle Rosaldo, "Toward an Anthropology of Self and Feeling," in Richard A. Shweder and Robert A. LeVine, eds., *Culture Theory: Essays on Mind, Self, and Emotion* (Cambridge: Cambridge University Press, 1984), 137–157, p. 139. For background to this paper, see also Michelle Rosaldo, *Knowledge and Passion: Ilongot Notions of Self and Social Life* (Cambridge and New York: Cambridge University Press, 1980); Renato Rosaldo, *Ilongot Headhunting, 1883–1974: A Study in Society and History* (Stanford, Calif.: Stanford University Press, 1980).

14. Hazel Markus and Paula Nurius, "Possible Selves," *American Psychologist* 41 (1986):954–969, p. 954. Nicholas Humphrey and Daniel Dennett, "Speaking for Ourselves: An Assessment of Multiple Personality Disorder," *Raritan: A Quarterly Review* (Spring 1989):68–98. Sigmund Freud, "The Relation of the Poet to Day-Dreaming," in *Collected Papers,* vol. IV, ed. Ernest Jones (London: Hogarth Press, 1950), 173-183.

15. Paul Ricoeur, "The Narrative Function," in Ricoeur, *Hermeneutics and the Human Sciences,* ed. and trans. John B. Thompson (Cambridge: Cambridge University Press, 1981), 277.

16. Carl Hempel, "The Function of General Laws in History," in

Hempel, *Aspects of Scientific Explanation and Other Essays in the Philosophy of Science* (New York: Free Press, 1942). Ricoeur again provides a succinct summary. Hempel argues, he notes, that "any singular events can be deduced from two premises. The first describes the initial conditions: antecedent events, prevailing conditions, etc. The second asserts a regularity, a universal hypothesis which, when verified, merits the name of law. If the two premises can be properly established, then the event under consideration can be logically deduced, and is said, thereby, to be explained." Ricoeur, "The Narrative Function," p. 275. Hempel admits, of course, that history has trouble establishing such premises, that it must work mostly with explanatory sketches. But that is not really the point. The point, rather, is whether sequences and plots are relevant to the historian's task. It is not only W. B. Gallie who objects, but such working historians as, say, Lawrence Stone, who sees the narrative form as one of history's central tools, arguing that history is descriptive and interpretive, rather than analytic and "explanatory." W. B. Gallie, *Philosophy and Historical Understanding* (New York: Schocken Books, 1964); Lawrence Stone, "The Revival of Narrative: Reflections on a New Old History," *Past and Present* 85 (1979):3–24. Stone insists, besides, that history must be involved in a "rhetoric" through which "pregnant principles" are argued as demonstrative in the particulars—as when Thucydides seeks to show the sequence of events through which the Peloponnesian War had disastrous effects on Greek society and *polis*.

17. Albert Lord, *The Singer of Tales,* Harvard Studies in Comparative Literature, 24 (Cambridge, Mass.: Harvard University Press, 1960). Northrop Frye, *Anatomy of Criticism: Four Essays* (Princeton: Princeton University Press, 1957). Ricoeur, "The Narrative Function," p. 287.

18. C. G. Jung, *Collected Works,* vol. 9, pt. I: *Archetypes and the Collective Unconscious* (New York: Bollingen, 1959).

19. Aristotle, *Poetics*, trans. James Hutton (New York: Norton, 1982). Ricoeur, "The Narrative Function," pp. 288, 292.

20. "A sign, or *representamen*, is something which stands to somebody for something in some respect or capacity. It addresses somebody, that is, creates in the mind of that person an equivalent sign, or perhaps a more developed sign. That sign which it creates I call the *interpretant* of the first sign. The sign stands for something, its *object*. It stands for the object, not in all respects, but in reference to a sort of idea, which I have sometimes called the *ground* of the representamen. 'Idea' is here to be understood in a sort of Platonic sense very familiar in everyday talk; I mean in that sense in which we say that one man catches another man's idea." C. S. Peirce, *Collected Papers of Charles Sanders Peirce*, vol. 2 (Cambridge, Mass.: Harvard University Press, 1960), 228.

21. Why the expectable or the usual should thus be endowed with "value" or legitimacy is an interesting question. Perhaps the most interesting answer has been offered by G. W. Allport, *Personality: A Psychological Interpretation* (New York: Henry Holt and Company, 1937), in his theory of "functional autonomy." He proposed that habits, once established, take on the role of motives: the seasoned sailor develops a desire to go to sea, and so on. William James makes the same point in his celebrated chapter "Habit" in *The Principles of Psychology* (Cambridge, Mass.: Harvard University Press, 1983). Emile Durkheim is probably making a similar point in proposing that a community's shared beliefs achieve not only "exteriority" but also constraint in the sense of regulating desire. Durkheim, *The Elementary Forms of the Religious Life,* trans. Joseph Ward Swain (New York: Collier Books, 1961).

22. Roger G. Barker, *Habitats, Environments, and Human Behavior* (San Francisco: Jossey-Bass, 1978).

23. H. Paul Grice, *Studies in the Way of Words* (Cambridge, Mass.: Harvard University Press, 1989).

24. Kenneth Burke, *A Grammar of Motives* (New York: Prentice-Hall, 1945). I am indebted to David Shulman of the Institute of Asian and African Studies of the Hebrew University of Jerusalem for pointing out what may be an ethnocentric bias in this account. He raises the interesting question whether Kenneth Burke's account of the rhetoric of narrative may not be too "homeostatic" to be universal. "One could imagine—well, in fact there's no reason to imagine, since examples do exist in India—a narrative that begins with an initial imbalance or disharmony, proceeds to resolve it, and then concludes by restoring the original problematic state. Closure would then be a restatement of some dynamic, perhaps spiralling cycle of transformation. What comes to mind is the *Sakuntala* of Kalidasa, the most famous drama in Sanskrit literature: while Sanskrit poetics handles this play in a different way (more stable and integrated closure), my own reading of it would be something like I've outlined here. Incidentally, the ramifications for cognition are explicitly brought to the surface in the final act of this work, where the protagonist compares his own mental universe to that of a man who, while staring at a real elephant that is standing right in front of him, says, 'This is *not* an elephant'; and only later, as the elephant begins to move away, does a slight doubt arise in his mind; until finally, when the elephant has disappeared, the man observes the footprints it left behind and declares with certainty, 'An elephant *was* here' " (personal letter, 15 December 1989). It may well be that Burke's "dramatism" could be conceived (as Shulman implies) as a circle or cycle and that, depending upon tradition, one could start at any point in the cycle, the only requirement being that the story run the full cycle round. For a further discussion of this point, see Victor Turner, *From Ritual to Theatre: The Human Seriousness of Play* (New York: Performing Arts Journal Publications, 1982).

25. Hayden White, "The Value of Narrativity in the Representation of Reality," in W. J. T. Mitchell, ed., *On Narrative* (Chicago: University of Chicago Press, 1981), 1–24.

26. Jerome Bruner, *Actual Minds, Possible Worlds* (Cambridge, Mass.: Harvard University Press, 1986).

27. Erich Kahler, *The Inward Turn of Narrative,* trans. Richard Winston and Clara Winston (Princeton: Princeton University Press, 1973).

28. Erich Auerbach, *Mimesis: The Representation of Reality in Western Literature,* trans. Willard R. Trask (Princeton: Princeton University Press, 1953).

29. Wolfgang Iser, *The Act of Reading: A Theory of Aesthetic Response* (Baltimore: Johns Hopkins University Press, 1978). Iser's more recent *Prospecting: From Reader Response to Literary Anthropology* (Baltimore: Johns Hopkins University Press, 1989) develops this point more fully.

30. Jean Mandler, *Stories, Scripts, and Scenes: Aspects of Schema Theory* (Hillsdale, N.J.: Lawrence Erlbaum Associates, 1984).

31. John Shotter, "The Social Construction of Forgetting and Remembering," in David Middleton and Derek Edwards, eds., *Collective Memory* (London: Sage Publications, 1990), 120–138.

32. The books in question, of course, are F. C. Bartlett, *Psychology and Primitive Culture* (Cambridge: Cambridge University Press, 1923), and his classic *Remembering: A Study in Experimental and Social Psychology* (Cambridge: Cambridge University Press, 1932). Mary Douglas makes her claim in her *How Institutions Think* (London: Routledge and Kegan Paul, 1987), p. 25.

33. Bartlett, *Remembering,* p. 255.

34. Cynthia Fuchs Epstein, *Deceptive Distinctions: Sex, Gender, and the Social Order* (New Haven: Yale University Press, 1988).

35. Bartlett, *Remembering,* p. 21.

36. Iser, *The Act of Reading.*

151

37. Marx cited by Oliver Sacks in his introduction to A. R. Luria, *The Man with a Shattered Mind: The History of a Brain Wound* (Cambridge, Mass.: Harvard University Press, 1987).

38. For a useful discussion of the limits of sense and reference in defining meaning, see Umberto Eco, Marco Santambrogio, and Patrizia Violi, eds., *Meaning and Mental Representations* (Bloomington: Indiana University Press, 1988).

39. See particularly Marco Santambrogio and Patrizia Violi, "Introduction," in Eco, Santambrogio, and Violi, *Meaning and Mental Representations,* 3–22.

40. Roy Harris, "How Does Writing Restructure Thought?" *Language and Communication* 9 (1989):99–106.

41. John L. Austin, *How to Do Things with Words* (Cambridge, Mass.: Harvard University Press, 1962). Ludwig Wittgenstein, *The Blue and Brown Books* (New York: Harper and Row, 1958). Wittgenstein, *Philosophical Investigations,* trans. G. E. M. Anscombe (New York: Macmillan, 1953).

42. H. Paul Grice, *Studies in the Way of Words* (Cambridge, Mass.: Harvard University Press, 1989). For a concise discussion, see Stephen C. Levinson, *Pragmatics* (Cambridge and New York: Cambridge University Press, 1983).

43. Bartlett, *Remembering.* Roger Schank and Robert Abelson, *Scripts, Plans, Goals, and Understanding* (Hillsdale, N.J.: Lawrence Erlbaum Associates, 1977), 70. T. A. Van Dijk, *Macrostructures: An Interdisciplinary Study of Global Structures in Discourse, Interaction, and Cognition* (Hillsdale, N.J.: Lawrence Erlbaum Associates, 1980), 233–235.

44. Elizabeth W. Bruss, *Beautiful Theories: The Spectacle of Discourse in Contemporary Criticism* (Baltimore: Johns Hopkins University Press, 1982). Iser, *The Act of Reading.* Philippe Lejeune, *On Autobiography,* trans. Katherine Leary (Minneapolis: University of Minnesota Press, 1989).

3. Entry into Meaning

1. David Premack and G. Woodruff, "Does the Chimpanzee Have a Theory of Mind?" *Behavioral and Brain Sciences* 1 (1978): 515–526.

2. Claude Lévi-Strauss, *Structural Anthropology* (New York: Basic Books, 1963).

3. See Chapter 2, note 20.

4. See, for example, Noam Chomsky, *Language and Mind* (New York: Harcourt, Brace and World, 1968).

5. The reader interested in pursuing this issue further is referred to the thoughtful accounts of, for example: Derek Bickerton, *Roots of Language* (Ann Arbor, Mich.: Karoma, 1981); Steven Pinker, *Learnability and Cognition* (Cambridge, Mass.: MIT Press, 1989); Dan Isaac Slobin, ed., *The Crosslinguistic Study of Language Acquisition*, 2 vols. (Hillsdale, N.J.: Lawrence Erlbaum Associates, 1985); Kenneth Wexler and Peter W. Culicover, *Formal Principles of Language Acquisition* (Cambridge, Mass.: MIT Press, 1980).

6. A sample of volumes stimulated by Austin's *How to Do Things with Words* would include Jerome S. Bruner, *Child's Talk: Learning to Use Language* (New York: W. W. Norton, 1983); Herbert H. Clark and Eve V. Clark, *Psychology and Language: An Introduction to Psycholinguistics* (New York: Harcourt Brace Jovanovich, 1977); M. A. K. Halliday, *Learning How to Mean* (London: Arnold, 1975); and P. M. Greenfield and J. Smith, *The Structure of Communication in Early Language Development* (New York: Academic Press, 1976).

7. See, for example, Robert A. Hinde, *Individuals, Relationships and Culture: Links between Ethology and the Social Sciences* (Cambridge: Cambridge University Press, 1987), and Frank A. Beach, ed., *Human Sexuality in Four Perspectives* (Baltimore: Johns Hopkins University Press, 1977).

8. J. S. Bruner and Carol F. Feldman, "Where Does Language Come From?" (review of Derek Bickerton, *The Roots of Language*), *New York Review of Books*, no. 29 (June 24, 1982): 34–36.

9. Nicholas Humphrey, *The Inner Eye* (Boston: Faber and Faber, 1986). Roger Lewin, *In the Age of Mankind* (Washington, D.C.: Smithsonian Books, 1988).

10. A. Whiten and R. W. Byrne, "Tactical Deception in Primates," *Behavioral and Brain Sciences* 11 (1988):233–273. R. W. Mitchell, "A Framework for Discussing Deception," in R. W. Mitchell and N. S. Thompson, *Deception: Perspectives on Human and Non-human Deceit* (Albany: State University of New York Press, 1986).

11. M. Chandler, A. S. Fritz, and S. Hala, "Small-Scale Deceit: Deception as a Marker of Two-, Three-, and Four-year-olds' Theories of Mind," *Child Development* 60 (1989):1263.

12. See, for example, J. W. Astington, P. L. Harris, and D. R. Olson, eds., *Developing Theories of Mind* (New York: Cambridge University Press, 1988).

13. This finding was originally reported by H. Wimmer and J. Perner, "Beliefs about Beliefs: Representation and Constraining Function of Wrong Beliefs in Young Children's Understanding of Deception," *Cognition* 13 (1983):103–128. It has been replicated many times. See Astington, Harris, and Olson, eds., *Developing Theories of Mind*.

14. Chandler, Fritz, and Hala, "Small-Scale Deceit," 1275.

15. M. Scaife and J. S. Bruner, "The Capacity for Joint Visual Attention in the Infant," *Nature* 253 (1975):265–266. George Butterworth and M. Castillo, "Coordination of Auditory and Visual Space in Newborn Human Infants," *Perception* 5 (1976): 155–160. A. Ninio and J. S. Bruner, "The Achievement and Antecedents of Labelling," *Journal of Child Language* 5 (1978):1–15.

16. Halliday, *Learning How to Mean*.

17. I am aware that the more usual claim is that grammatical forms are mastered according to their "syntactical" or "computational" simplicity—the shallower the derivational depth or the simpler the computation, the easier learned. For one view see Kenneth Wexler and Peter W. Culicover, *Formal Principles of Language Acquisition* (Cambridge, Mass.: MIT Press, 1980); for another, Steven Pinker, *Language Learnability and Language Development* (Cambridge: Cambridge University Press, 1984). Such an idea may be formally attractive, but all examples thus far proposed exhibit the same fatal flaw. There is no way of establishing "simplicity" or "computability" independently of one's theory of grammar or computation. The test of the "theory," accordingly, is self-determined by the theory one is testing. The general effort is reminiscent of the early effort to establish the greater "simplicity" of "untransformed" sentences as compared to those "transformed" by negative, passive, or query transformations—the simpler requiring less mental processing time than the more complex. Not only were the predictions wrong; they were deeply and incorrigibly so. They failed, for example, to take context into account in their view of "sentence processing" and could not even begin to explain why negatively transformed sentences, encountered in a "context of plausible denial," were much more quickly comprehended than ordinary, untransformed indicative ones of the same number of elements. See P. C. Wason, "The Contexts of Plausible Denial," *Journal of Verbal Learning and Verbal Behavior* 4 (1965):7–11. Also see Nelson Goodman's discussion of "simplicity" in his *The Structure of Appearance* (Cambridge, Mass.: Harvard University Press, 1951).

18. Roger Brown, *A First Language: The Early Stages* (Cambridge, Mass.: Harvard University Press, 1973).

19. At least one distinguished linguist, Charles Fillmore, has even

gone so far as to speculate that case grammar in terms of which language is organized—the familiar classes of agent, action, patient, object, direction, location, and the like—is an abstract linguistic rendering of some prior conceptual grasp of the "arguments of action" that serve to organize our experience about human activity. See Charles Fillmore, "The Case for Case," in E. Bach and R. T. Harms, eds., *Universals in Linguistic Theory* (New York: Holt, Rinehart, and Winston, 1968), 1–88, and Fillmore, "The Case for Case Reopened," in P. Cole and J. M. Sadock, eds., *Syntax and Semantics: Grammatical Relations,* vol. 8 (New York and London: Academic Press, 1977), 59–81.

20. See, for example, J. S. Bruner, "Pacifier-Produced Visual Buffering in Human Infants," *Developmental Psychobiology* 6 (1973): 45–51. William Kessen, P. Salapatek, and M. Haith, "Visual Response of Human Newborn to Linear Contour," *Journal of Experimental Child Psychology* 13 (1972):9–20. I. Kalnins and J. S. Bruner, "The Coordination of Visual Observation and Instrumental Behavior in Early Infancy," *Perception* 2 (1973):307–314. Kathleen M. Berg, W. Keith Berg, and Frances K. Graham, "Infant Heart Rate Response as a Function of Stimulus and State," *Psychophysiology* 8 (1971):30–44.

21. "Markedness," in *Selected Writings of Roman Jakobson,* vol. 8, ch. 2, pt. 4 (Berlin, New York, Amsterdam: Mouton De Gruyter, 1988). Greenfield and Smith, *The Structure of Communication in Early Language Development.*

22. Willem J. M. Levelt, *Speaking: From Intention to Articulation* (Cambridge, Mass.: MIT Press, 1989). Joseph H. Greenberg, ed., *Universals of Human Language* (Stanford, Calif.: Stanford University Press, 1978). Brown, *A First Language.*

23. Daniel N. Stern, *The First Relationship: Infant and Mother* (Cambridge, Mass.: Harvard University Press, 1977). See also Olga K. Garnica, "Some Prosodic and Paralinguistic Features

of Speech to Young Children," in Catherine E. Snow and Charles A. Ferguson, eds., *Talking to Children: Language Input and Acquisition* (Cambridge and New York: Cambridge University Press, 1977), 63–88, and Ann Fernald et al., "A Cross-Language Study of Prosodic Modifications in Mothers' and Fathers' Speech to Preverbal Infants," *Journal of Child Language*, in press.

24. A. R. Luria, *The Role of Speech in the Regulation of Normal and Abnormal Behavior* (New York: Liveright, 1961). Margaret Donaldson, *Children's Minds* (New York: Norton, 1978). V. Propp, *The Morphology of the Folktale* (Austin: University of Texas Press, 1968).

25. Chandler, Fritz, and Hala, "Small-Scale Deceit."

26. Personal communication.

27. Peggy J. Miller, *Amy, Wendy, and Beth: Learning Language in South Baltimore* (Austin: University of Texas Press, 1982). Peggy J. Miller and Linda L. Sperry, "The Socialization of Anger and Aggression," *Merrill-Palmer Quarterly* 33 (1987): 1–31. Peggy J. Miller and Linda L. Sperry, "Early Talk about the Past: The Origins of Conversational Stories of Personal Experience," *Journal of Child Language* 15 (1988):293–315. Peggy J. Miller, "Personal Stories as Resources for the Culture-Acquiring Child," paper presented at Society for Cultural Anthropology, Phoenix, Arizona, November 18, 1988.

28. See Peggy J. Miller and Barbara Byhouwer Moore, "Narrative Conjunctions of Care-Giver and Child: A Comparative Perspective on Socialization through Stories," *Ethos* 17, no. 4 (1989):428–449. The narrative form in question was first described by W. Labov and J. Waletzky, "Narrative Analysis: Oral Versions of Personal Experience," in J. Helm, ed., *Essays in the Verbal and Visual Arts* (Seattle: University of Washington Press, 1967), 12–44.

29. Shirley Brice Heath, *Ways with Words: Language, Life, and*

Work in Communities and Classrooms (Cambridge and New York: Cambridge University Press, 1983).

30. Miller and Moore, "Narrative Conjunctions of Care-Givers and Child," 436.
31. Heath, *Ways with Words*.
32. Judy Dunn, *The Beginnings of Social Understanding* (Cambridge, Mass.: Harvard University Press, 1988), p. 5.
33. Kenneth Burke, *A Grammar of Motives* (New York: Prentice-Hall, 1945).
34. John L. Austin, "A Plea for Excuses," in Austin, *Philosophical Papers,* 2nd ed. (Oxford: Clarendon Press, 1970), 175–204.
35. Katherine Nelson, ed., *Narratives from the Crib* (Cambridge, Mass.: Harvard University Press, 1989).
36. Vladimir Propp, *Theory and History of Folklore,* trans. Ariadna Y. Martin and Richard P. Martin (Minneapolis: University of Minnesota Press, 1984).
37. Ruth Weir, *Language in the Crib* (The Hague: Mouton, 1962).
38. Labov and Waletzky, "Narrative Analysis."
39. Carol Fleisher Feldman, "Monologue as Problem-solving Narrative," in Nelson, ed., *Narratives from the Crib.*
40. Michelle Rosaldo, *Knowledge and Passion: Ilongot Notions of Self and Social Life* (Cambridge and New York: Cambridge University Press, 1980).
41. Frans de Waal, *Peacemaking among Primates* (Cambridge, Mass.: Harvard University Press, 1989).
42. Milan Kundera, *The Book of Laughter and Forgetting,* trans. Michael Henry Heim (New York: Alfred A. Knopf, 1980). Kundera, *The Unbearable Lightness of Being,* trans. Michael Henry Heim (New York: Harper and Row, 1984). Danilo Kis, *A Tomb for Boris Davidovich,* trans. Duska Mikic-Mitchell (New York: Harcourt Brace Jovanovich, 1978).
43. Ronald Dworkin, *Law's Empire* (Cambridge, Mass.: Harvard University Press, 1986). For further adumbration of the role

of narrative in the law, see *Michigan Law Review* 87, no. 8 (August 1989), an issue given over entirely to the topic of "Legal Storytelling." I am particularly indebted to Martha Minow of the Harvard Law School for bringing this work to my attention, and also to Peggy Davis, David Richards, and Tony Amsterdam of the New York University Law School for discussing its significance with me.

4. Autobiography and Self

1. Edwin G. Boring, *The Physical Dimensions of Consciousness* (New York: Dover, 1963).
2. The "realism" of Self is probably built into folk psychology as a spinoff of the notion of agency. It is surely built into English language usage, though in a strikingly idiosyncratic way. We say "Control yourself." But we do not say "bring yourself to dinner next Wednesday." And typically, we permit Self to be both subject and object of sentences with mental as with action verbs: It is permissible to say that "you cut yourself," where the final term conventionally translates into some part of the body; but it is equally permissible to say "you doubt yourself," which after all is a tall order of folk metaphysics for a language to accept without cavil. The middle case is occupied by such expressions as "I hurt myself" rather than simply "I hurt." But in this instance the two forms are usually used to distinguish the punctate from the durative. So far as I have been able to determine, there has been no fully systematic study of the linguistic and cognitive prerequisites for the use of personal pronouns as reflexive predicates. One is surely needed. But for some interesting reflections on the embodiment of self-realism in such usage, see Peter Strawson, *Individuals* (London: Methuen, 1959); George A. Miller and Philip N. Johnson-Laird, *Language and Perception* (Cambridge, Mass.: Belknap Press of Harvard Uni-

versity Press, 1976); and Bernard Williams, *Problems of the Self* (Cambridge: Cambridge University Press, 1973).

3. William James, *Principles of Psychology* (New York: Macmillan, 1890).

4. See Hazel Markus and Paula Nurius, "Possible Selves," *American Psychologist* 41 (1986):954–969. Other, somewhat similar models of self have been proposed. Examples include Anthony R. Pratkanis, Steven J. Breckler, and Anthony G. Greenwald, eds., *Attitude Structure and Function* (Hillsdale, N.J.: Lawrence Erlbaum Associates, 1989); Robbie Case, *Intellectual Development: Birth to Adulthood* (Orlando: Academic Press, 1985); Tory E. Higgins, "Self-Discrepancy: A Theory Relating Self and Affect," *Psychological Review* 94 (1987):319–340.

5. It is well instantiated in the work of Richard Rorty: *Consequences of Pragmatism* (Minneapolis: University of Minnesota Press, 1982); *Philosophy and the Mirror of Nature* (Princeton: Princeton University Press, 1979). The "sleeper effect" of Nietzsche's perspectivalism is discussed in Alexander Nehamas, *Nietzsche: Life as Literature* (Cambridge, Mass.: Harvard University Press, 1985). But the impact of perspectivalism on psychology also stems from the antirealism in Ernst Mach, *The Analysis of Sensations, and the Relation of the Physical to the Psychical* (Chicago: Open Court, 1914). Karl Popper's skepticism also had a strong impact—e.g., *Objective Knowledge: An Evolutionary Approach* (Oxford: Clarendon Press, 1972)—as of course did Thomas Kuhn's discussion of paradigm shifts in science in *The Structure of Scientific Revolutions* (Chicago: University of Chicago Press, 1962). My own generation even had a "cult text" on the matter: Hans Vaihinger's *The Philosophy of 'As If': A System of the Theoretical, Practical, and Religious Fictions of Mankind*, 2nd ed., trans. C. K. Ogden (London: Routledge and Kegan Paul, 1935). Percy Bridgman's operationism also went a long way toward undermining the simplistic naive realism of

earlier science: *The Logic of Modern Physics* (New York: Macmillan, 1927).

6. George Herbert Mead, *Mind, Self, and Society* (Chicago: University of Chicago Press, 1934).

7. One may note the parallel development of this idea in the work of Mikhail Bakhtin on "heteroglossia"—*The Dialogic Imagination: Four Essays,* ed. Michael Holquist (Austin: University of Texas Press, 1981)—and of Lev Vygotsky on the "internalization" of dialogue in the creation of "inner speech" and thought—*Thought and Language* (Cambridge, Mass.: MIT Press, 1962).

8. Ruth C. Wylie, *The Self-Concept,* vol. 1: *A Review of Methodological Considerations and Measuring Instruments* (Lincoln: University of Nebraska Press, 1974); vol. 2: *Theory and Research on Selected Topics* (Lincoln: University of Nebraska Press, 1979). Also Wylie, *Measures of Self-Concept* (Lincoln: University of Nebraska Press, 1989).

9. K. Lewin, T. Dembo, L. Festinger, and P. Sears, "Level of Aspiration," in J. McV. Hunt, ed., *Personality and the Behavior Disorders* (New York: Ronald, 1944).

10. See Clark L. Hull, *Principles of Behavior* (New York: Appleton-Century, 1943); Edward C. Tolman, *Purposive Behavior in Animals and Men* (New York: Appleton-Century, 1932).

A comparably deep division separated those theories of learning which fall under the rubric of "conditioning." Pavlov studied salivating in harnessed dogs who had just heard a sound or light that presaged delivery of a bit of food. That came to be called "classical conditioning." B. F. Skinner, rejecting such a passive approach, introduced the idea of an "operant response"—a pigeon pecking, say, at a button discriminately marked one way when it would deliver a grain of corn, and not so marked when it would not. Skinner's operant and Pavlov's classical conditioning, of course, yield very different pictures of what learning is like. The former is replete with inhibition and disinhibition, spread of excitation, and so on. The latter concerns itself with the conditions that increase or decrease the likelihood of a response.

Karl Zener demonstrated that if you let Pavlovian dogs out of their harness and let them wander about the laboratory, the onset of conditioned salivation was quite different from the way it had been found to work in the rigid conditions of the Moscow Institute. If getting back to the food tray required some tricky detouring, for example, the dogs seemed to have other things than salivating on their "minds." Then Hobart Mowrer demonstrated that classical and operant conditioning operated under different conditions, the former for autonomically mediated behavior, the latter for more "voluntary" responses.

It was to Tolman's credit that he eventually published a classic paper entitled "There Is More than One Kind of Learning," *Psychological Review* 56 (1949):144–155. But the "paradigm locking" persisted, for each theorist conceived the *basic* form of learning to be the one generated by his or her experimental paradigm, with the upsetting exception to be "explained away."

The distinction between "map room" and "switchboard" theories is discussed in Tolman's "Cognitive Maps in Rats and Men," *Psychological Review* 55 (1948):189–208.

11. Typical studies of this type include those reported in Neal E. Miller, "Experimental Studies in Conflict," in J. McV. Hunt, ed., *Personality and the Behavior Disorders* (New York: Ronald, 1944); and such specific research studies as O. Hobart Mowrer, "Anxiety Reduction and Learning," *Journal of Experimental Psychology* 27 (1940):497–516; Edward C. Tolman, "A Stimulus-Expectancy Need-Cathexis Psychology," *Science* 101 (1945): 160–166; John Dollard and N. E. Miller, *Personality and Psychotherapy* (New York: McGraw-Hill, 1950).

12. A typical example from this period was George A. Kelly's two-volume *The Psychology of Personal Constructs* (New York: Norton) which appeared in 1955, a year before the by-now-standard date for the "opening" of the cognitive revolution. I reviewed it in *Contemporary Psychology* 1, no. 12 (1956):355–358, and hailed it as the first "effort to construct a theory of personality from a theory of knowledge: how people come to know the world by binding its diverse appearances into organized construct systems" (p. 355).

13. See Roy Pea and D. M. Kurland, "On the Cognitive Effects of Learning Computer Programming," *New Ideas in Psychology* 2 (1984):137–168; R. Pea, "Distributed Intelligence and Education," in D. Perkins, J. Schwartz, and M. M. West, eds., *Teaching for Understanding in the Age of Technology* (in preparation); D. N. Perkins, "Person Plus: A Distributed View of Thinking and Learning," paper delivered at the Symposium on Distributed Learning at the annual meeting of the A.E.R.A., Boston, April 18, 1990. While the notion of distributed learning has, as it were, been around for a long time—anthropologists particularly have been mindful of it as, too, has Michael Cole, as in his "Cultural Psychology: A Once and Future Discipline," in J. J. Berman, ed., *Nebraska Symposium on Motivation, 1989: Cross-Cultural Perspectives* (Lincoln: University of Nebraska Press, forthcoming)—the idea has been given new force in its application to man's relation to new informational technologies. See, particularly, John Seeley Brown, Alan Collins, and P. Duguid, "Situated Cognition and the Culture of Learning," *Educational Researcher* 18:32–42.

14. Ann L. Brown, "Distributed Expertise in the Classroom," paper delivered at the Symposium on Distributed Learning at the A.E.R.A., Boston, 1990. For a fuller account of this work, see also Ann Brown and Joseph Campione, "Communities of

Learning and Thinking: Or a Context by Any Other Name,"
Human Development, forthcoming. The quotation is from Perkins, "Person Plus," p. 24.

15. Of course it was also contextual considerations that shut down
the amphitheater of "animal learning" in which battles over
learning theory were classically fought. The ethologists made it
clear that in an evolutionary sense learning was geared to particular conditions in the environments of particular species. It
could not be treated in isolation, separate from habitats and
from instinctual predispositions that had been selected in evolution to match those habitats. Learning, whatever form it might
take, was always biased and filtered in terms of those predispositions which had been selected by evolution, and one could not
take account of it without specifying a great deal more than
that an animal was "exposed" to a particular environment. So
again, learning and the learner could not be isolated from the
animal's habitat or, for that matter, from the evolutionary history that had made the habitat "adaptive" to the animal's predispositions. See, particularly, Niko Tinbergen, *The Animal in Its
World,* vols. 1 and 2 (London: George Allen and Unwin, 1972,
1973).

16. I do not mean to imply that the idea of "distributive" thinking
had been absent from psychology altogether. Vygotsky had
some such notion in mind in his formulation of pedagogy and
in the role he assigned history in the shaping of thought (see
his *Thought and Language*). David Wood and I were also grop-
ing for a way of characterizing the "scaffolding" of intellectual
activity that takes place in knowledge exchanges: Wood,
Bruner, and Gail Ross, "The Role of Tutoring in Problem
Solving," *Journal of Child Psychology and Psychiatry* 17
(1976):89–100. And a distributional view early characterized
the work of Michael Cole and Sylvia Scribner, e.g., *Culture and
Thought: An Introduction* (New York: Wiley, 1974).

17. Karl Joachim Weintraub, *The Value of the Individual: Self and Circumstance in Autobiography* (Chicago: University of Chicago Press, 1978); E. R. Dodds, *The Greeks and the Irrational* (Berkeley: University of California Press, 1951); Michelle Rosaldo, *Knowledge and Passion: Ilongot Notions of Self and Social Life* (Cambridge and New York: Cambridge University Press, 1980); and Fred Myers, *Pintupi Country, Pintupi Self* (Washington: Smithsonian Institution Press, 1986). Four volumes of *A History of Private Life* have been published to date by Harvard University Press: the first in 1987 under the editorship of Paul Veyne, *From Pagan Rome to Byzantium*; the second in 1988 by Georges Duby, *Revelations of the Medieval World*; the third in 1989 by Roger Chartier, *Passions of the Renaissance*; the fourth in 1990 by Michelle Perrot, *From the Fires of Revolution to the Great War*. One more is in preparation.

18. Lee J. Cronbach, *Designing Evaluations of Educational and Social Programs* (San Francisco: Jossey-Bass, 1982), p. 108.

19. See Kenneth J. Gergen, *Toward Transformation in Social Knowledge* (New York: Springer-Verlag, 1982), pp. 17ff. The original research is reported in several papers referred to in that volume, particularly Gergen and M. G. Taylor, "Social Expectancy and Self-Presentation in a Status Hierarchy," *Journal of Experimental Social Psychology* 5 (1969):79–92; and S. J. Morse and K. J. Gergen, "Social Comparison, Self-Consistency, and the Presentation of Self," *Journal of Personality and Social Psychology* 16 (1970):148–159.

20. Gergen, *Toward Transformation in Social Knowledge*, p. 18.

21. Gergen, of course, was influenced in this view by Bartlett's *Remembering*, discussed in Chapter 2.

22. Kenneth Gergen, "Social Psychology as History," *Journal of Personality and Social Psychology* 26 (1973):309–320.

23. I do not say this critically. One of the objectives of the early cognitive "revolutionaries" was to replace the mindless image

of man that had emerged during the long reign of behaviorism. Indeed, I was among those rationalists, as witness the central importance of the concept of strategy in Bruner, J. J. Goodnow, and G. A. Austin, *A Study of Thinking* (New York: Wiley, 1956).

24. Among the critical publications that set the climate for that period were, surely, the following: W. J. T. Mitchell, ed., *On Narrative* (Chicago: University of Chicago Press, 1981); Paul Rabinow and William Sullivan, eds., *Interpretive Social Science: A Reader* (Berkeley: University of California Press, 1979); Clifford Geertz, *Interpretation of Cultures* (New York: Basic Books, 1973); Richard Rorty, *Philosophy and the Mirror of Nature* (Princeton: Princeton University Press, 1979); and the writings of such French post-structuralist critics as Roland Barthes and Michel Foucault.

25. Donald Spence, *Narrative Truth and Historical Truth: Meaning and Interpretation in Psychoanalysis* (New York: Norton, 1984). As a matter of historical interest, it is very plain that Roland Barthes had a strong influence on Spence's formulation: his word is cited in support of Spence's central idea of the role of alternative codes in interpretation.

26. Spence intends by "code" something approximating Roland Barthes's idea of various semiotic codes, discussed at length in Barthes's book *Image, Music, Text* (New York: Hill and Wang, 1977), codes that extract different kinds of meanings from a text. But Spence was by no means trying to expunge from psychoanalysis the idea of "real" or "archaeological" memories. Narrative truths, rather, represent (in the classical psychoanalytic sense) compromises that result from "the conflict between what is true and what is tellable" (*Narrative Truth*, p. 62). Indeed, Spence's stand on the "reality" of untellable memories suggests that, while he is a "heuristic constructivist" where memory is concerned, he is by no means willing to give up a

positivist's belief in the existence of "real" memories. This places him in an anomalous position with respect to classic psychoanalysts who, in the main, accuse him of jettisoning the "reality" of an id in which traumatic memories are stored, indeed, like well-preserved archaeological specimens.

27. Spence, *Narrative Truth*, p. 63.

28. David Polonoff, "Self-Deception," *Social Research* 54 (1987): 53. A view very similar to Polonoff's is also widespread in contemporary autobiographical theory. For a particularly lucid exposition of it, see Janet Varner Dunn, *Autobiography: Toward a Poetics of Experience* (Philadelphia: University of Pennsylvania Press, 1982).

29. Roy Schafer, "Narration in the Psychoanalytic Dialogue," in W. J. T. Mitchell, ed., *On Narrative* (Chicago: University of Chicago Press, 1981), p. 31.

30. Ibid., p. 38.

31. See, for example, the collection of papers in Theodore G. Sarbin's edited volume *Narrative Psychology: The Storied Nature of Human Conduct* (New York: Praeger, 1986). A striking instance of this new approach is contained in Michelle Rosaldo's *Knowledge and Passion*, discussed in Chapter 2. In certain respects, this new "interpretivist" trend can be traced back to George Herbert Mead, particularly to his *Mind, Self, and Society* (Chicago: University of Chicago Press, 1934). But in certain other respects, Mead was so wedded to the classic late-nineteenth-century view of the interaction of "organism" and "environment" that it is better, in my opinion, to consider him as a closing chapter on conceptualism in the late history of positivism than as an opening chapter in the new interpretivism. See, for example, Mead's discussion of "Organism, Community, and Environment" in *Mind, Self, and Society*, pp. 245ff.

32. Clifford Geertz, "From the Native's Point of View: On the Nature of Anthropological Understanding," in P. Rabinow and

W. M. Sullivan, eds., *Interpretive Social Science* (Berkeley: University of California Press, 1979), pp. 225–241, quotation on p. 229. It is interesting that a decade later E. E. Sampson begins a discussion entitled "The Deconstruction of the Self" with Geertz's rejection almost as an epigraph: see Sampson in John Shotter and Kenneth Gergen, eds., *Texts of Identity* (London: Sage, 1989).

33. A recent and excellent example is Sidonie Smith, *A Poetics of Women's Autobiography: Marginality and the Fictions of Self-Representation* (Bloomington: Indiana University Press, 1987).

34. See Elliot G. Mishler, "The Analysis of Interview-Narratives," in Theodore R. Sarbin, ed., *Narrative Psychology: The Storied Nature of Human Conduct* (New York: Praeger, 1986). For a fuller account of some of the techniques used in analyzing such interview-narratives, see Mishler, *Research Interviewing: Context and Narrative* (Cambridge, Mass.: Harvard University Press, 1986).

35. Donald Polkinghorne, *Narrative Knowing and the Human Sciences* (Albany: SUNY Press, 1988), p. 150.

36. Psychologists, even quite philosophically sophisticated ones, have always been extremely chary of "historical explanation." I think this chariness stems from a common misconception about the difference between "explanation" in the causal sense discussed in the first two chapters, and "interpretation" in the historical or cultural sense. An interesting contrast is provided by two psychologists of the past generation—Kurt Lewin and Lev Vygotsky. In a celebrated essay entitled "Aristotelian and Galilean Modes of Thought"—see his *Dynamic Theory of Personality* (New York: McGraw-Hill, 1935)—Lewin condemns historical "causation" as necessarily "teleological" and as involving "action at a distance." What determines behavior *now* is what is present in the "behavioral field" of the individual actor at the time of action. This "Galilean" idea was, in his view, the source

of the great success of the physical sciences. Doubtless there is a sense in which the same ideal would be relevant to the human sciences—that we should not invoke "tradition" without some specification of how the tradition in question is *represented* in the hearts and minds of the participants in an act going on here and now. But the manner in which an enduring tradition operates to define and alter meanings in the here and now is *not* the same as the way in which a field of forces reflects the resultants of physical events that created it.

Vygotsky, of course, followed a quite different route. He proposed that the method of psychology, however experimental and empirical it might become, was necessarily "cultural-historical" at its root. For the tools and instruments that human beings employ in the "enablement of mind" are essentially cultural tools that were transformed historically by the circumstances of social and economic life. Their history reflects itself, therefore, in the nature of their use now. It is of no small interest that Lewin, contemplating emigration from Germany when fascism was on the rise, visited Vygotsky in Moscow with an introduction from his Russian student Zeigarnik; see Guillermo Blanck, *Vygotsky* (Buenos Aires: in preparation; personal communication, October 1989). Unfortunately, there is no record of their conversation, although it is reported that they got on famously in spite of the enormous difference in their attitudes toward the role of history in psychological interpretation.

37. In an as yet unpublished study, I had more than a dozen readers interpret this story while in the process of reading it for the first time, and I think I know most of the interpretations offered by critics as well. Interpretations, for all their diversity, share one overwhelmingly important characteristic: they are *all* efforts to invoke an intentional state (a motive or state of mind) in the captain/protagonist. The more sophisticated among the readers

also tried to understand how the story was emblematic of our culture, or of Conrad's plight in that culture.

38. See, for example, Ellen Langer, *The Psychology of Control* (New York: Sage, 1983).

39. Philippe Lejeune, *On Autobiography* (Minneapolis: University of Minnesota Press, 1989), p. 132.

40. Dr. Weisser and I are now completing a volume on this work to be published by Harvard University Press, entitled "Autobiography and the Construction of Self." It goes without saying that a different way of approaching the interview would have produced different ways of telling. If, for example, one asks people to tell about "memories of the past," one is much more likely to obtain lists of recalled events, with much less of an accounting of what these events "mean" to the teller. For other ways of going about the task of eliciting a record of the past from human subjects, see David C. Rubin, ed., *Autobiographical Memory* (Cambridge: Cambridge University Press, 1986).

41. Mishler, *Research Interviewing*. This issue is better left for fuller discussion in Bruner and Weisser, "Autobiography and the Construction of Self."

42. Keith Thomas, review of Roger Chartier, ed., *A History of Private Life,* vol. 3, *New York Review of Books,* 9 November 1989, p. 15. The volumes in this series are among the great accomplishments of the French *Annales* school of historians. Perhaps the best known of these historians among psychologists was Philippe Ariès, whose *Centuries of Childhood: A Social History of Family Life* (New York: Knopf, 1962) argued that the concept of childhood was a "social invention" rather than a fact, and that it was constantly being reshaped. The position taken by the *Annales* historians, beginning with one of its founders, Lucien Febvre, has been that "privacy" is to be understood as a "spin-off" from post-medieval sociopolitical arrangements rather than as an expression of some basic psychological or biological need.

Subject Index

171

Name Index

Note: Where an author is mentioned in the text with an accompanying endnote, only the appropriate text page is referenced in the index, not the endnote. When authors are mentioned only in the endnotes, the appropriate endnote will be found referenced in the index.